The Greatest
HUMAN
DECEPTION

Sidiah Veronica Audifferen
and Samuel Akinola Audifferen

ARPress

ARPress
45 Dan Road Suite 5
Canton MA 02021
Hotline: 1(888) 821-0229
Fax: 1(508) 545-7580

Ordering Information:

Quantity sales. Special discounts are available on quantity purchases by corporations, associations, and others. For details, contact the publisher at the address above.

Printed in the United States of America.

ISBN-13:   Softcover   979-8-89330-866-2

             eBook   979-8-89330-867-9

Library of Congress Control Number: 2024902476

Table of Contents

Summary

The Greatest Human Deception is certainly one of the most explosive thought-provoking books of immense proportions and dimensions. Certainly, a "Christian Classic" and a must-read book beneficial to all. Using indisputable scientific facts, the author diagnoses the reasons for world problems of health, hatred with wars, and provides the "magic" prescription to cure all individuals and world problems. Argues forcibly that the present educational system of the world is flawed because it is in the "wrong direction," and advocates a "turn around" to the "right type of education." An inspiration to believers, an eye-opener to unbelievers, a challenge to atheists, agnostics, and the uncommitted. In *The Greatest Human Deception*, the existence of God is not an exercise of "Quod Erat Faciendum" but a magnificent and colossal statement of "Quod Erat Demonstratum" (that which has been proven or demonstrated). A grand philosophical edifice, cemented with scientific facts.

About the Author

Born in Nigeria of French/German and Swiss roots, a product
of King's College, Lagos, Nigeria; gained various certificates
in Biblical Studies. Immigrated to Glasgow, Scotland. Obtained
Bachelor of Science degree at the University of Paisley, Scotland,
and graduated as a certified teacher from St. Andrews College of
Education with "Merit in Teaching." For almost two decades, he was
Head of the Biology Department in the Scottish High School, during
which period, he spent a few years reading for Ph.D. He successfully
contributed to the development of Scottish Examination Board
courses within the science field. Represented the Baptist Union of
Scotland in the British Council of Churches from 1976 to 1989, and
the Baptists in the Glasgow Council of Churches from 1985 to 1989.
Relocated to the United States of America where he read and gained
Master of Science degree majoring in Educational Leadership.
Continued education took him to various universities in U.S.A.

Dedication Area

This page is dedicated to all the true servants of God and the Lord Jesus Christ, past, present, and future.

Audifferen's Concepts

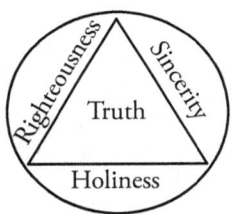

Acknowledgments

Many thanks to Miss Amanda Porto of Alonso High School, Tampa. Florida who helped in typing the first two chapters of this book. Thanks to Mrs. Donna Hignite who for a short period helped, and my gratitude and thanks to Ms. Brenda Bowden for making the manuscript ready and for her invaluable suggestions. My thanks also to Ms Landers of Garland V. Stewart Middle Magnet School, Tampa, Florida for the creation of the copyright logo of Audifferen's Concepts.

Special Thanks

My special thanks to my faithful wife and partner,
SIDIAH VERONICA, for the faith, courage, love, and hope
displayed when we pass through the difficulties and joys of life.

Thank you Sidiah for your faithful services,
friendship, companionship, and Love.

Introduction

There are various misconceptions and deceptions of man across the ages, in all the environments and cultures of man, but the greatest human deception is the most fatal and catastrophic, beyond the realization and comprehension of man. The greatest human deception is an attempt to present the whole picture of the glories and follies of man in a panoramic way, designed to capture the imaginations of all and trigger thought-provoking exercises that expose deceptions in the face and light of the truth. History tends to repeat itself in a cycle reminiscent of the present, past and the anticipated future. Where do we begin our journey? What is life or the meaning of life? What is man? What is the goal of man or the goal of life? Is there a connection between life, peace and health? Despite the great advancements made in the medical field, why is it that man has not been able to eradicate diseases? Why is it that we have suffering all over the world and the education of man is powerless to arrest the situation? Why do we have hatred in the world, racial bias, and a big division between the rich and the poor? "Why, can't we all get along?" was the famous question asked by Rodney King. What is the root of all the problems of mankind? Are there solutions to all of these problems? Is mankind deceived and being deceived? Is mankind in rebellion and in the face of facts clinging to fantasy and on collision course? The purpose of this book is to reach every human being of every culture, color, tribe, and affiliation, in every corner of this planet earth.

The importance of this message to every human being is paramount to life, peace, and sound health. It is the sincere hope and prayer of the author that the millions or billions of people who will either read this book or hear the message of this book and believe will come into the enlightenment of the truth in the face of scientific facts and everyday common knowledge. A great prophet who eight hundred years before the occurrence of the most significant event on this planet earth accurately and succinctly described step by the step the sequence of events that will lead to the culmination and fulfillment of his prophecy asked in frustration, " Who hath believed our report?"

The writer hopes that on the release of this book, he would not have to repeat the question of that famous prophet, "Who hath believed our report?" For those who are not students of history and may be wondering who the prophet was, it was prophet Isaiah who almost eight hundred years before the birth of our Lord and Savior Jesus Christ described in various chapters of his book the birth and the suffering of Christ. Beginning with the birth of Jesus, Isaiah, eight hundred years before the event, foretold His birth, His deity, His ministry, His death, and His future millennial reign. Every item predicted has been fulfilled but the last, His future millennial reign. Whoa! The book dances with science, religion, philosophy, sociology, genetics, and humanities. The writer presents indisputable scientific facts and explores understanding beyond the limitations of existing knowledge to promote the ideology of peace, using scientific facts rooted in genetics to support, consolidate, and prove beyond any reasonable doubt the "Theory of the Brotherhood of Man" under the ancestry of his original parents. It is the first book to reveal the "Code of Ownership" of man by His maker in the figure eight of the human circulatory system.

Friends and readers, you see that the Holy Bible is not a collection of fairy tales compiled by zealots in order to cow down some people. The birth of Jesus is the most significant event on the planet earth because it concerns every human being on this planet. Why? Every human being has a part of God in him or her which is the spirit of existence because God is the universal spirit of all flesh. David, king of Israel and Prophet of God, in Psalm 24, tells us that "The earth is the Lord's and the fullness thereof, the world, and theywho dwell therein." The point is compelling. Whether you believe it or not does not change the truth and fact that "everybody is born into this world and everyone will die in this world." From this truth, you will appreciate the earlier sentence that the birth of the Lord Jesus Christ is the most significant event that has occurred so far on this earth planet. Therefore, Christmas should be a day of joy, rejoicing, and thanksgiving to God for His incomparable gift to humanity.

Let us go back now to the remarkable predictions and prophecies of Isaiah, bearing in mind that he wrote down those prophecies almost eight hundred years before the event. He wrote in Isaiah 9:6 (King James Version), "For unto us a child is born, unto us a son is given, and the government shall be upon his shoulder; and His name shall be called "Wonderful, Counselor, The Mighty God, The Everlasting Father, The Prince of Peace." In Isaiah 7:14, he wrote as follows: Therefore, the Lord Himself shall give you a sign, behold the virgin shall conceive, and bear a son, and shall call his name "Immanuel," God with us. Who was the mother of Jesus? A virgin, named Mary. The significance of the birth of Jesus can be fully appreciated only when we look at the free benefits granted to mankind:

1) Jesus is the "missing link" back to God.

2) Jesus is the "bridge" between God and man.

3) Jesus is the "peace-maker" between God and man.

4) Jesus is the power and wisdom of God to man.

5) Jesus breaks down the walls and barriers that separate God and man. Jesus paid the full debt for man, redeemed, and ransomed man from ignorance, the second or spiritual death, and restored man back to God.

6) As He died on the cross, we read in Matthew 27:51 that "The veil of the temple was torn in two from the top to the bottom" thereby ushering in for us the benefits of direct contact with God in the Holy of Holies.

7) Man lost God in the Garden of Eden, or rather man is lost and has been lost since Eden. It is because man lost God that he admits himself that he is lost, and life is meaningless to him because he is lost. The good news is that Jesus looked for lost man, found him, and restored him to God.

8) Jesus bestows on man the Holy Spirit of God since the Day of Pentecost.

9) Jesus suffered on the cruel cross to set mankind free from the curse.

10) Jesus makes mankind debt free and sealed our pardon.

11) Jesus delivered us from the power of darkness, and witches as well as wizards testify to the mighty delivery power of Jesus when his name is pronounced.

12) We have redemption through the blood of Jesus, the forgiveness of sins.

13) As our High Priest and mediator before God, Jesus presents us holy and blameless and above reproach before our Heavenly Father.

14) Jesus Christ is in every believer, and He is the Hope of Glory.

15) Jesus wiped out the ordinances against us, took them out of the way and nailed them to the cross.

16) For our benefit, Jesus disarmed principalities and powers. He made a public spectacle of them, triumphing over them.

17) Jesus makes us to be sons and daughters of the Living God.

18) Jesus makes us to be kings and priests of the Living God

19) Jesus makes us to be co-heirs with Him.

20) Jesus offers us eternal life through His death.

21) Jesus Christ gives us a "second birth" so that we are born again, of the Spirit of God and are being led by the Holy Spirit as we surrender ourselves to the guidance of the Holy Spirit.

22) Finally, Jesus bestows on us eternal blessings of God that are beyond the imagination and comprehension of man, because "Eye has not seen, or ear heard" the great things God has prepared for us through Christ Jesus.

Is the Environment the Determinant
of Education and Destiny?

From the microenvironment to the macroenvironment, from the dwellers at mountain tops to the inhabitants of valleys, from the richest to the poorest, from kings to peasants, free men to slaves, education is not only intrinsically linked and wedged; it shapes, controls, and determines the direction of the individual, community, populations, and nations of the world.

In human beings, education is not only an essential tool but the director of important services, while the environment to some extent is the determining factor in the outcome of the individual. The popular and acceptable view of the masses is that education is the key to success and happiness in life. It is believed that your education provides you with a passport to unlimited opportunities of life. It is not, therefore, surprising that down through the ages, the rich and the wealthy have sent their children to the best institutions and colleges of the time, while the poor have struggled or languished in the murky and muddy waters of poverty. The end result is a pyramid whereby the masses are at the bottom and the educated few at the top. That led to all forms of social problems and of division of the society between the few learned elite of the society at the top and the illiterate masses at the bottom of the pyramid, thus perpetrating a gap between the rich and the poor. Soon, it became obvious to all that everyone needs education, and there was a change in attitude.

There are those born in palaces. They are assured of a good education and life. There are those born in homes of the rich and famous, and, if they are obedient to their parents, they too are assured of a good education and comfortable lives because they are "born with silver spoons." There are those born in the poor villages, in the ghettos, and poorest homes, and they may struggle and have no college education because of their environment of poverty. Nevertheless, the truth is that whether they are born in palaces, in the homes of the rich and famous, in the poor villages, in the ghettos, or in the poorest homes, they are all born "ignoramus;" and all must go through the process of learning. Does this hint to us that the purpose of life is education? Moreover, everyone born has an appointment with "death the leveler," who puts all mankind on the same plane and level, whether black or white, yellow, or pink, rich or poor. As one of the poets puts it, "There is no armor against fate, death lays its icy hands on all."

However, it is significant to note that the right type of education leads to accomplishment, joy, success, happiness, and sometimes peace of mind. On the other hand, the wrong type of education leads to disobedience, rebellion, suffering, hardship, wars, and hatred. History has shown that the education received by any population, community, or nation affects the sociology, culture, progress, or decline of that nation. We shall deal with this later.

It is fascinating to observe that science has confirmed what the Holy Bible says about learning. Where does learning begin? Scientific research has confirmed that learning begins in the womb as the fetus knows and identifies the voice of his or her mother. The child in the womb of the mother does much more than simply hear sounds, including the mother's voice. Science now agrees that life in the womb is nothing less than a normal stage of human existence. This is one of the reasons abortion is ethically wrong because it tantamount to murder. Where do babies come from? Our grandparents and great grandparents tell us that babies come from Heaven, but that answer amuses high school students in a biology class. The high schoolers look at the visible and tangible evidence and declare that babies come as a result of the union of a man and a woman during an act of sexual intercourse resulting in pregnancy and producing ababy or babies as the case may be. Who is right? Or what is right? From secular science's point of view, the high schoolers are right, but are our grandparents wrong? Are our great grandparents wrong? Do great grandparents and grandparents have the ultimate knowledge and insight that looks at the whole picture, whereas our high schoolers see part of the picture and assume it is a whole picture?

Let us look at the scientific fact of the high schoolers and compare it with the affirmations of our grandparents that babies come from Heaven. The scientific fact is that during "fertilization," the union of the sperm of the man and the egg or ovum of the woman, the resulting zygote (which will develop into a baby) receives half of the characteristics of the father and half of the characteristics of the mother. The resulting fetus will have 23 pairs of chromosomes. This brings us to the sex determination of the baby. According to science, the mother has XX chromosomes, and the father has XY chromosomes, so that the Y chromosome determines the sex of the baby. If the resulting baby has XY chromosomes, he is a boy, and XX chromosomes, a girl. The chromosomes or the DNA of the baby contains the " map" of the baby, boy or girl, black or white or yellow, tall or short, blood group "0" or "A" or "AB," and so forth. Therefore, the appearance of the baby (what biologists call phenotype) is known from the genotype (the genetic constitution) of the baby. This confirms that "out of the invisible (genotype) comes the visible appearance (phenotype)." Does this not remind us of one of the attributes of God given to us by Prophet Isaiah in chapter 46:10 of his book? "God declares the end from the beginning and from ancient times, the things that are not yet done, saying, "My counsel shall stand, and I will do all my pleasure" (Isaiah 46:10).

If we go back to the arguments of the high schoolers and the grandparents, we see that the axis tilts in favor of the grandparents who say that babies come from Heaven when we look at the whole picture. The sexual act that produced the baby did not design the baby. It was only the physical act, the visible part. The invisible part initiated the physical act. The beauty of the woman that attracted the husband is an invisible force that magnetized both of them. God, the Giver of Life, took over and designed the DNA of the new arrival into the family. Both husband and wife do not know what was going on in the formation of the baby. They do not know whether the baby will be tall or short when he grows up, but all that information is in the DNA from the conception. This is an undeniable fact and confirms the truth of God's word that He "declares the end from the beginning." There are historical facts that attest to our findings. We learn from history that one hundred years before Cyrus, King of Persia, was born, the God of Abraham, Isaac and Jacob, the God of Isaiah declared the time Cyrus would be born, his sex (male), and the name that Cyrus would be called. Not only that, but God also declared the mission of Cyrus to perform God's will and release the Jews. In the face of these facts, we see that our grandparents are right when they tell us that babies come from Heaven. Our grandparents gave a spiritual answer because they had the ultimate knowledge that the spiritual (invisible) produces the physical (visible) entity. Babies do come from Heaven as the example of Cyrus shows: but a better example is that of the Lord Jesus Christ whose birth was foretold almost eight hundred years before.

The environment where a baby is born plays a significant part in the journey of the baby through life. History shows that babies born in Christian homes may become Christians, those born in Islamic homes may become Muslims, those born in India may become Hindus or Sikhs, those born in Sri Lanka, Tibet or China may be Buddhists, those born in Japan may become "Shinto" worshippers, and, to some extent, the microenvironment also plays an equally important role in the development of the baby. If the baby is born in a rich home or poor home, in a palace or in a shanty house, the course of the baby can be charted. All the babies of the world, there-fore, come from the same place from Heaven. All are born naked into the world whether they are rich or poor, princes or princesses. We can, therefore, begin to understand the wisdom of God and see the foolishness of man who oppresses his brother or sister, on the basis of race, color, tribe, and poverty, in contrast to God who is not a respecter of persons but accepts all who fear Him, work righteous-ness, and walk uprightly. How does the individual baby arrive at the family in which he finds himself? This is surely a topic beyond the scope of this chapter but is mentioned to stimulate deep and critical thinking.

Ladies and gentlemen, the purposes of life have already been revealed to us by God, but we tend not to see them or understand them. One of the purposes of life given to us by God is responsibility with education. When the little baby arrives at the family, it is the responsibility of both father and mother to look after the baby, take care of the baby, protect the baby from dangers, love the baby, and teach the baby, who is born an "ignoramus," the environment in which the baby finds himself or herself. The first lesson given to the baby is the language of communication and identification of the surroundings. We point out "Daddy" and "Mommy" to the baby. The baby learns who the mother is and who the father is. The baby is gifted with certain instincts that he or she can identify the mother and father also on his or her own through the "sense of smell" of various items, including "blood". Though learning begins in the womb, the baby continues to learn about the environment when he is born into this world. We send this baby to school and to college. In every station of life, there is continuity of learning actively or passively, voluntarily or involuntarily because of the structure and function of the brain and mind of man. Therefore, the purpose of life is education. After receiving all this education, we see the third purpose of life, service to mankind. Whether we are physicians, surgeons, lawyers, administrators, teachers, computer wizards, or any imaginable profession, we render services to our fellow men. The purposes of life are, therefore, responsibility, education, service, and worship. All the four purposes are linked: but education and worship are intertwined in that they lead us to the ultimate purpose of life which is to know the one and only True God, the Mystery of all Mysteries, the Father of Truth and Light, the Eternal Wisdom of the Ages, who wants us to know Him through the means of the right type of education.

Some people have the misconception that religion is a limiting factor that hinders the advancement of knowledge and science. The writer says emphatically that it is absolutely untrue. How could it be true when the Creator and Maker uses science and technology in all His works? David, the King of Israel, tells us in Psalm 19, that the "Heavens declare the Glory of God; and the firmament shows his handiwork." Who among us is not impressed by the stars that are suspended in space? Who among us is not amazed at Mount Everest? Who is not enthralled by the Niagara Falls and the oceans of the world? Who is not confounded by the beauty of the works of creation? We are ruled by beauty, and beauty inspires us to reach the unreachable sky. It is the beauty of a woman that makes a billionaire prepared to spend whatever it costs to have her as a wife. Nowadays, the beauty of beautiful women is used in selling cars, merchandise, homes, and all the ramifications of life. We have become idolatrous in that we worship beauty instead of the Creator of beauty. Women spend thousands of dollars to have plastic surgery to make them look prettier, younger and delicious. This shows the magnification of the "culture of beauty." Is this the new type of education sweeping the affluent society? What we fail to realize is that the importance of education in the success of life depends on what type of education is being given or received. Are we giving children the right type of education? As we have read earlier, the home is the first station of education and not the schools. Do we do what is wrong in the presence of our children and underestimate their intelligence? Bearing in mind that the ultimate purpose of life is to know the one and only True God through the means of the right type of education, we must realize that discipline is part and parcel of our responsibility: and if we fail to apply appropriate discipline, everything falls apart. The question, therefore, is how we differentiate the right type of education from the wrong type of education? This question leads us to a very complex area in which the aims of education are linked up with the purpose of education and surrounded by the inevitable questions of what life is, what is the meaning of life, and what is the purpose of life? We have already seen that every human being is born an "ignoramus" who has to learn everything he or she knows. That shows us that education is a life-long journey. "We learn everyday of our life" is indeed a very old saying. We read earlier that there is a difference between the right type of education and the wrong type of education. The product of each type of education contributes to or determines the culture, characteristics, religion, and probably the stability of the government of the people. This is how pivotal education is to the societies and the nations of the world.

Every history student can tell us that civilization began in Africa

(Egypt); and today in the 21" century, there are those who devote their time studying "Egyptology." It is very fascinating to know that for over 3,000 years, kings and courtiers built lavish tombs at Saqqara, the national cemetery of kings who settled at the city of Memphis. Egyptian kings and people prepared for eternity from the onset of their lives. My friends and readers, are you preparing for eternity? The education given to the Egyptians was that life everlasting begins with a journey from the tomb through the underworld. They claimed that "life force" or the Ka, leaves the body first, followed by the Ba, or soul. "Horns," a falcon-headed god, then leads Ba through door-ways of fire and cobras into the hall of judgment. In the hall of judgment, Anubis, the jackal-headed god weighs the deceased's heart, site of the conscience, against the feather of "maat" or things as they should be. Osiris, king of the underworld, and other gods watch as judges. If the heart is too heavy or too light, a monster that is part lion, part crocodile and part hippopotamus devours it, dooming the deceased to a perpetual coma. If the heart balances, the winged Ba and the Ka reunite to form an "akh" or spirit which emerges in the bright realm ruled by crowned Osiris. The "akh" can now re-enter the living world and enjoy its pleasures, including his wife's love and the attention of his servants. The education of the kings and the wealthy was that life is a preparation for eternity. This idea of life being a preparation for eternity is, in a sense, equivalent to the tenet of the Christian faith. It is gratifying to note that in Germany certain thinkers — Kant, Herbart, Lotze and Froebel — said that it is necessary to believe in God; therefore, the knowledge of God is the principal knowledge and the chief end of education. A salute to these great German thinkers! The author agrees very strongly with the German thinkers that the chief end of education is the knowledge of the one and only True God. He is completely different from all the other gods through the manifestation of His glory and power. He makes light to travel at 186,000 miles per second and the heart of man to beat at 72 times a minute. He is the greatest scientist of all ages, and He wants us to know Him and His science. Contrary to misconception and deception of some, He is a God of Progress, and He wants us to progress. God does not keep anyone back. Religion did not rule the dark ages. Men's wicked hearts ruled the dark ages. Because of the rebellion of man, the philosophy of the German thinkers was not embraced. So, what happened? Others propounded different ideas. One thesis says, "Education is true science of relations" and the object of education is to put a child in living touch with as much as may be of the life of nature and of thought. Nel Noddings, Professor Emeritus at Stanford University argues that "The main aim of education should be to produce competent, caring, loving, and lovable people." Seymour Sarason says, "The overarching purpose of schooling is to stimulate, capitalize on, and sustain the kind of motivation, intellectual curiosity, awe, and wonder that a child possesses when he or she begins schooling." Alfie Kohn says the purpose of education is not primarily to help children know more; rather, it is to help children become better able to think, care, imagine, understand, and adapt — to become autonomous learners. History shows that at the onset of education, schools were designed to teach children routine skills and to "facilitate the memorization of important texts, principally religious ones," with which everyone was already acquainted. Some argue that traditional practices such as direct instruction, fact-based tests, and a quest for the right answer are more consistent with the original conception of school whose catechisms "sought to produce believers rather than thinkers." Jean Piaget believed that "The principal goal of education is to create men and women who are capable of doing new things, not simply repeating what other generations have done — men and women who are creative, inventive, and discoverers who have minds which can be critical and verify (rather than) accept everything that are offered." It was said that Woodrow Wilson, during his tenure as President of Princeton University, stood before a roomful of high school teachers and announced, "We want one class of persons to have a liberal education, and we want another class of persons, a very much larger class of necessity in every society, to forgo the privilege of liberal education and fit themselves to perform specific difficult anual tasks." The question is asked, "Do we want schools to be about sorting people out, the presumed able from the less able or about educating all children, generously and without qualification?" It appears that since the founding of America, the nation has been of two minds about this matter. Through various arguments and discussions about education, two camps emerged —The camp of "education for democracy" and the camp of "education for profits." The former argues that schools should be equipping students with the skills they will need to maintain, sustain, or create a democratic society. The latter camp says that schools should be preparing students to be productive workers in order to sustain a booming economy. The economic justification for schooling appears to go hand in hand with the Wilsonian vision of separating the privileged from the peons, adequately skilled laborers who will do their part to increase the profitability of corporations. Looking around in the 21st century at the ongoing debate about the purposes of education, business interests appear to have gained the tipper hand.

Conflicting ideas about the aims and purposes of education are tossed about relentlessly. There is the humanistic approach to education, based on a solid foundation of psychological theory and research, in which the center of gravity is shifted back to the student. Thrown into the arena is "constructivism," a philosophical position which calls into question not only traditional ideas of knowing and learning but also our understanding of knowledge itself, especially the idea that the world to be known is "out there," independent of people, waiting to be taken in. Constructivists argue that reality, including scientific phenomena, are construed and ultimately constituted by us as much as they are observed. "Science, like history, literature, and other fields, is not the story of the world impinging on us but of constructs that have been invented and imposed on phenomena in attempts to interpret and explain them, often as results of considerable intellectual struggles" (Driver et al, 1994, 6). Associated with the philosophy of "constructivism" are such approaches as whole language, fuzzy math, and invented spelling,as well as a disdain for phonics and grammar, insistence that there are no right answers (just different ways to solve problems), and an emphasis on students' self-esteem. Constructivists dislike any kind of ability grouping or special classes for children. By diminishing the authority of the teacher, constructivist methods often create discipline problems.

Other educators believe that learning depends on the efforts of both highly skilled teachers and students, that students need self discipline more than self-esteem, that accuracy is important, that in many cases there truly are right answers and wrong answers (the Civil War was not caused by Reconstruction), and that instructional methods should be chosen because they are effective, not because they fit one's philosophical values.

We see from the different views and ideas of education that it is an ongoing process for all, particularly in this information age. The television commercials designed to enlighten us about products and to sell materials to us affect our lives in various ways, especially those advertising products dealing with health issues. We see the impact of education on the public because the commercials raked in billions of dollars of sales of drugs and other materials to corporations. We have read the different shades of opinion on education, but the author is convinced that basically there are two types of education: the right type of education and the wrong type of education. The author believes that the right type of education is given to us by the wisest human being who lived on this planet earth, Solomon. Solomon says to us in Proverbs 1:7 that "The fear of the Lord is the foundation of knowledge." The children of Israel were commanded to bring up their children in the "knowledge and admonition of the Lord." The phrase "knowledge and admonition of the Lord" quickly brings into view the characteristics of the Lord God – holy, righteous, eternally good, just, true, light, upright, unmovable, unchanging, faithful, kind and loving. This point is very essential to society because if children are raised up to be truthful, honest, kind, merciful, just, loving, forgiving and sharing, they will develop characteristics of "Holiness;" and such a society will have little or controlled crime. This is the right type of education that leads to peace, sound health, joy, and lasting happiness. Isn't it time we went back to the basics and started teaching values such as honesty, love, and character to our children? In the 2004 American Presidential election, twenty-two percent of voters put "moral values" at the top of their list, surpassing terrorism, the war in Iraq, health care, economics and other key issues. Those moral values were advertised conspicuously in eleven states where, by overwhelming margins, Americans affirmed marriage as a union between one man and one woman. This is how it has been ordained from the beginning of time when God Himself performed the marriage ceremony for Adam and Eve in the Garden of Eden.

In the author's view, there is a wrong type of education because history shows that whenever the wrong type of education super-cedes the right type of education, society experiences upheaval, calamity, instability, corruption, moral decadence, wickedness, and evil, all of which eventually lead to the downfall or overthrow of the government. The wrong type of education is ill-defined, sometimes narrow-minded, often too broad-minded, with parameters of liberalism, painted with uncertainties and inundated with dogmas. One classic example is the "little red book" of chairman Mao of China and the remarkable influence of this little red book in the lives of the Chinese people in the 20th century. The education of the people was geared to the promotion of the ideas of communism and the contents of the "little red book." Consequently, communism became the political bastion of the nation. However, the end result was the collapse of communism because it did not meet the reality of life in that philosophical theories are incompatible with the practicalities of life. It is, therefore, evident that, in a world created by the Eternal God, evil cannot last but only stands for a limited period of time before the forces of goodness overtake it.

At the collapse of communism, yesterday's heroes become today's villains when the eyes of the people were opened to the truth. In this example, we see the role of education in the life of the nation and the effect of that type of education on the life of the individual.

Propaganda, effectively mustered, can become a form of education for the people; and the life of everyone in the nation may be affected. History tells us this in another case study of skillful political propaganda presented in the form of education to the people.In the 1920's and 1930's, Adolf Hitler propounded the theory of the "Aryan Blood;" and in his book Mein Kampf, he gave theoretical examples of the purity of the "Aryan Blood" and the supremacy of the Aryan blood. He wrote that "All the human culture, all the results of art, science, and technology that we see before us today arealmost exclusively the creative product of the "Aryan." The claims made of the "Aryan Blood" are false and deceptive because they are diametrically opposed to the fact and truth of life. It is because of the rebellion of man to God that man clings to every false theory since he rejects the truth of God; but the Holy Scripture says, "Let God be the true and all men liars."

The true knowledge of blood was given to us two thousand years ago when the Rev. Doctor St. Paul spoke to the greatest, ablest, highest intellectuals of Europe on Mars Hill. The truth and the fact is "God has made of one blood all nations of the earth (Acts 17:26).

In the face of scientific facts, man finds it difficult to accept truth and, thereby, succumbs to deception. Jesse Owens, the African-American athlete of the 1936 Olympic Games, proved Hitler's Aryan's blood theory false when he captured four gold medals to the fury of Hitler. Instead of revising his theory, Hitler became angry because his monopolistic idea was openly discredited. Instead of reconciling himself to the truth, Hitler pursued his Aryan Blood Theory and precipitated the Second World War in which millions lost their lives. Millions of Jews were sent to the gas chambers from concentration camps. Why on earth did this happen? There are certain facts to ponder before drawing a conclusion. One of the facts is that Hitler was democratically elected because he won the elections before he became the Furher or President of Germany, which means that the majority of the Germans at that time supported the Theory of the Aryan Blood and the supremacy of one race over all others. Therefore, the education provided by Hitler through the power of his book Mein Kampf was accepted and believed by the majority of Germans.

It is very ironical and axiomatic that the Germans who are so clever, gifted, and talented did not perform "acid tests" on the contents of the book. The book, in point of fact, confirms the truth of the scriptures. Analysis of the book shows every grievance or objection raised against the Jews is really a confirmation of the Truth of God declared in the Holy Bible. Hitler wrote that "The Jews of all time lived in the state of other people." This is true because the Bible says, "God scattered them to every nation of the world;" so, in France you find the Jew as a Frenchman, or in England anEnglishman, in Germany a German, or in Italy an Italian, and so on. The fact is that there are Jews in every nation of the world, and this confirms the judgment of God on the Jews that He would scatter them if they were disobedient to His Laws and Ordinances. In like manner, it can be argued that the existence of the Jews is a confirmation of the existence of God. In Mein Kampf, Hitler wrote that "The Jew comes as a merchant and, with his dexterity, the Jew is far superior to native merchants." What? Wait a minute! How and where does the Jew acquire dexterity in business? Is it innate? Is it the blessing of Abraham, Isaac, and Jacob? Is it the finger of God in their commercial activities? Another grievance of Hitler against the Jews was that "He lends money at usurious interest." Surprising or news? This type of activity was one of the reasons the Jews were scattered. God told them in His word not to charge usurious interes to their brethren, but they did and disobeyed their God, hence their dispersal across the globe. One emergent fact is that there are only a few Jews, yet they control the finances and commerce of the nations of the world. Why is this so? The fact of the matter is that the blessing of God first pronounced on Abraham, Isaac, and Jacob is with the Jews: and it was a pity that Hitler and those who embraced his book did not read or understand the Holy Scriptures. The "Aryan Blood Theory" is contrary to the truth and fact that God has made of one blood all nations of men. For this reason, it is easy to understand the universal brotherhood of man first propounded by our Lord Jesus Christ and expanded for us by St. Paul. Although little or no attention was paid to the veracity of the remarkable and epic speech of Paul on Mars Hill, it did not change the truth that all men are made of one blood, as science has since discovered, proving the nucleus of St. Paul's speech. The amazing thing is that Hitler and many Germans did not remember the scientific work and discovery of Karl Landsteiner. Karl Landsteiner was an Austrian-born American scientist who in the 1900's discovered the A, B, 0 blood group system, the M, N, and P systems in 1927; and the rhesus system in 1940. Therefore, there are basically, within the human population, four blood groups a person can belong to: A, B, AB, or 0, depending on the presence or absence of Antigens A and B carried on the surface of one's red blood cells. Group A has the A antigen, Group B has the B antigen, Group AB has both antigens, and Group 0 has neither antigen. Also present in the blood plasma are antibodies that act against antigens not present on a person's own red blood cells. Group A blood contains anti-B antibodies, Group B blood contains anti-A antibodies, Group 0 blood contains both antibodies, and Group AB blood contains neither.

Undoubtedly, the blood group tells us that the "designer" of life is wisdom, knowing fully well that blood is the life of human beings. If we turn to the compatibility of the blood group, we arrive at the truth of the declaration of the Lord Jesus Christ that all men are brothers. If we consider the implication of that declaration, it means a black man can receive blood transfusions to save a life of a white man and vice-versa. In view of this fact, one is apt to ask why there is hatred or bitterness between the races of men? The observation of the writer is that man rejects the truth of God that all men are brothers; consequently, bitterness, envy, sufferings, murders, wickedness, evil, greed, and hatred abound in the lives of people. In order to fully grasp the significance of the brotherhood and sisterhood of man, let us look at the diagram showing the compatibility of the blood group showing the donor and the recipient. How can anyone look at this diagram and not sigh in wonder? Why does man reject the truth?

Is it because this knowledge does not satisfy the desires for power, wealth and greed? Wherever the path of true education is forsaken, dogmas, falsehood, deceptions, hatred and evil take over the feelings and emotions of men. Despite the scientific knowledge provided by Landsteiner, Adolf Hitler proceeded with his plans and, consequently, World War II was precipitated.

It is, therefore, not surprising that Simon Sebag Montefiore, author of Stalin, wrote that "Almost everyone would agree that Hitler, Stalin and MAO were among the greatest monsters in human history and that Osama Bin Ladin is the brutal Islamo-fascist enemy of everything we hold dear." He added that they are peerless villains that have become brand names of demonology. They were fanatical believers in a creed that included mass murder to make a better world. He continues by saying that politics was their superlative interest, and everything was subordinated to and poisoned by politics.

COMPATIBILITY OF THE BLOOD

DONOR

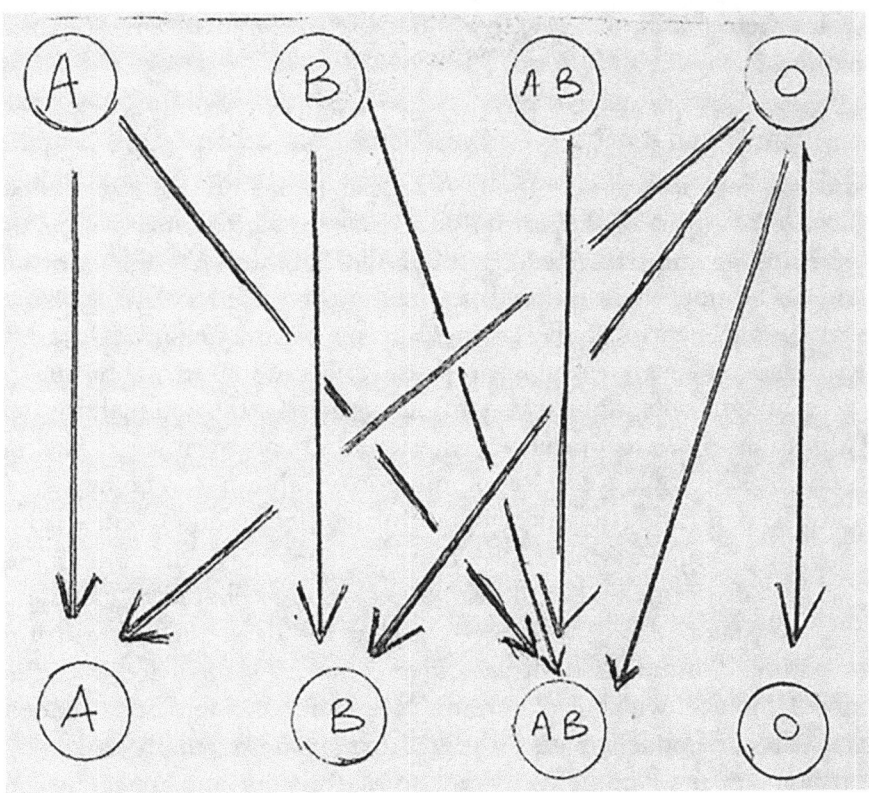

RECIPIENT

We can infer that these people received, acclaimed and propagated the wrong type of education. We have seen how the wrong type of education has affected millions of people, and we cannot just discard the notion of the wrong type of education as a joke. Let us look at another case study of the wrong type of education and its consequences which were felt all over the world because of the involvement of the nations in the Second World War.

During World War II, the ancient Japanese religion was "Shinto." Shinto is a rich mixture of folklore, reverence for all things natural, and the Japanese nation itself. A special brand of state-sanctioned "Shinto" was the ideological foundation upon which Japan's emperor worshipping military machine was built. "Shinto" has no scripture and no founder; hence, it is different from the major religions of the word. Its treatment of the Japanese people as unique and divine, its emphasis on harmony, and its deep-seated fear of impurity continue to be an integral, albeit not always conscious, part of the national psyche. "Shinto" has been stripped of its official status in post-war Japan, having been tarnished by the excesses of militarism. "Shinto" has no dearth of gods. Its pantheon is poetically said to have eight million deities from Amaterasi Omikami (the sun goddess) to Konohana Sakuya Hime (the goddess of Mount Fuji). All dead ancestors are believed to assume a god-like status. Along with reverence for the dead and the worship of nature, "Shinto" is built around a complex body of folklore, the most famous of which explains how Japan's imperial family descended from the sun goddess. Due to the fact that Japan is regularly shaken by earthquakes and hammered by typhoons, dispelling and appeasing the gods are also crucial aspects of "Shinto." Shrine festivals are big events nationwide, signifying the type of education received by the nation. Tens of millions of Japanese visit their local shrines on the first three days of each year. There are more than 80,000 shrines, but not all have a resident priest.

"Shinto" was the only government sanctioned religion, used to rally the nation behind modernization and militarization. Under state "Shinto," the divinity of the emperor and the special place of the Japanese people became official dogma. Thus, we see what the wrong type of education bequest to a great nation. The realizationof the wrong type of education always comes late. However, there has been a change in direction. The late Emperor Hirohito publicly renounced the idea that he was a living god. A new constitution for the nation was enacted, and it ensured freedom of religion and the separation of church and state.

The coronation of Hirohito's son, Emperor Akihito, climaxed in 1990 with the ancient ceremony in which the monarch is believed to commune with the sun goddess, from whom the "Shinto" establishment still claims he is a direct descendant. Akihito's priests continue to observe rituals at three shrines behind the moat of the Imperial Palace. Just outside the moat lies Tokyo's Yasukuni Shrine, the site of vociferous dispute over "Shinto's" place in Japan culture. Synonymous with nationalism, Yasukini was built in the late 1800's as a monument to Japan's military might and a memorial to its fallen soldiers. Howls of outrage from across Asia and several constitutional challenges to official patronage have not stopped political leaders from regularly bowing before its altar. Why? Is it because the stigma of fear rules in the hearts of the people? Oh! That people may come into the right type of education and learn that "Perfect love casts out fear."

Apartheid: Another Wrong Type of Education

Another wrong type of education which the world has known is apartheid, acceptable in South Africa from 1950-1990. Apartheid was a system of laws and regulations in existence for more than forty years in South Africa, separating the races by force. South Africa earned the nickname "The Rainbow Nation" on account of its diverse population which was comprised of Black Africans 76.2%, White African 12.8%, Colored (Mixed African and White Ancestry) 2.6%, and Zulu 22%.

South Africa is the world's leading producer of gold with annual extraction representing more than a quarter of the world's total. South Africa is also the fifth largest producer of diamonds including nearly 10% of the world's quality gemstones.

Because of the wrong type of education, South Africa is still feeling the legacy of centuries of oppression and discrimination against its black population. Inequalities in wealth were madeworse by a legacy that denied most people the chance to own land, work, vote, or even live where they chose in South Africa. It is not yet known by all that in a world created by God, evil cannot last though it may stand for a brief period of time. It was not, therefore, surprising that after forty years (1950-1990), apartheid crumbled; and an unjust government that oppressed its own people through poverty and misery was buried.

One of the most harmful deceptions of man is racism; and as we see in "apartheid," it is a product of the wrong type of education. At recurrent intervals throughout history, human beings have tended to despise and dislike people they saw as different from themselves. The difference might be one of language, religion, social class, or the color of their skin; that is, physical appearance and characteristics. Racism grows out of this hostility or contempt for the people who are "different." It is suggested that St. Peter the Great Apostle of Jesus Christ may have been a racist until the day he visited Cornelius, a centurion of the Italian Band, with all the Gentiles present with him in his house. Peter opened his mouth and said, "Of a truth, I perceived that God is no respecter of persons; but in every nation, he that feareth God, and worketh righteous-ness is accepted with Him." Peter witnessed the outpouring of the Holy Spirit of God on the Gentiles, and he adjusted his thinking and actions. Did mankind learn anything from that experience and the testimony of Peter? The answer is negative because of deception. Racists believe that their own culture is superior to others because mankind prefers falsehood to truth, darkness to light, and hatred to love. Racism affects societies in a range of practical ways — people are denied educational opportunities and jobs and suffer the day-to-day humiliation of being regarded as different and inferior. In the USA, Eugene Florence, a black man wanted to become a preacher of righteousness in the 1940's. He attended seminary at night because black students weren't allowed 'to take day classes. In 2004, fifty-three years after Eugene graduated with a theology degree, 100-year-old Eugene Florence was awarded a Masters of Divinity degree at South Western Baptist Theological Seminary. Officials said they we're correcting the injustice he endured at the segregated institution. Patterson, the seminary president admitted that "The previous race policy, which barred black students from receiving master's degrees, was unbiblical, ungodly, and un-Christian in every way." Let us look at another example. In February 1939, the Daughters of the American Revolution refused Marian Anderson the right to sing at Constitutional

Hall in Washington, D.C. Miss Anderson was known then as a Negro (black) contralto who had sung for audiences worldwide. When the news reached the First Lady, Eleanor Roosevelt, she resigned from the organization, thereby setting the pace for sisterhood of all ladies, American in particular, and of the world in general. Miss Anderson excelled at operatic arias and spirituals. Conductor Arturo Toscanini judged her voice to be "one that comes in a hundred years."

Ofcourse, white people have not been the only people in history to feel racial superiority. Arabs had a long tradition of black slavery, which they justified by seeing Africans as inferior beings. This, again, is one of the deceptions of man. It is an affront to God for anyone to say that a human being designed and created by God is an inferior being. That statement does not equal to scientific tests and findings. If the brains of those so called inferior human beings could have been examined then, scientists would have found what later scientists discovered only in the 1980's, "stochastic resonance." Scientists have now confirmed that our brains have built-in "stochastic resonance" much more sophisticated than the units scientists even dream of building someday. This is another blow in the cheek to the "theory of evolution." Is it not sad to know that some African people felt superior to other African peoples and dominated and exploited them? Some Japanese still believe that they belong to a naturally superior race and look down on other Asians. We see, therefore, that the rejection of the truth of God that all nations and races of men are made of one blood and are, there-fore, brothers and sisters in the family of God, a truth confirmed by science through the work of Karl Landsteiner, is a disaster for all. Just think of what lovers of falsehood participate in. In the United States, white supremacists, Christian identity adherents, skinhead groups, and other extremists are citing the events of September 11, 2001, to recruit new members, especially young people. Their message is one of falsehood enveloped in deceit and stamped with hatred. This is the wrong type of education, and the new wave of white supremacy must be countered with truth and scientific facts to eradicate falsehood impregnated with deception. From what has been written, we see the suffering and misery that the wrong type of education has brought to the nations of the world. Therefore, there must be an overhaul of all the wrong types of education and a new beginning. Science and the latest scientific discovery has certainly opened a new chapter of enlightenment and eradication of racism if people believe science.

The present course of man is precarious. A new direction must be pursued. At least in the United States and most of the Western World, sex has become the goddess of destruction but has masqueraded as the pinnacle of enjoyment. The present type of education which the secular world gives has sunk to the lowest depth of depravity and has ushered in sickness and diseases unmanageable and uncontrollable by man. The home is the first station of learning from the parents, and God holds the parents responsible for the upbringing of children. My friends, learn this eternal truth — the children are not your children "per se." They are God's children, given to you, entrusted to you as blessings from God. Therefore, when you, as a parent, fail to bring them up properly as they should be, the onus of responsibility lies squarely on your shoulders; and you will be accountable to God for them.

Overhaul of the Wrong Type of Education: Starting from the West to the Entire World.

The world in general, as a result of the rejection of the one and only True God, has pursued the wrong type of education, especially in the so-called western civilization; and the consequences of the wrong type of education have been broken marriages and families, sexual perversion, abortion (which is murder), alcoholism, greed, selfishness, disobedience to parents, disrespect of adults and senior citizens, wickedness, and murder. There must be an overhaul of the liberalism, laxity, and permissiveness, disguised, masqueraded and paraded as life styles which have almost destroyed the fabric of many societies in many countries of the world with AIDS, HIV,sexually transmitted diseases, and a host of other deadly diseases unmanageable and uncontrollable.

The school curriculum must be changed or modified from grade 3 to 12 and into the colleges and universities of every state of America and in other nations. College is included because in the USA, spring holidays are synonymous with heavy drinking, sex and orgies. It is, therefore, not surprising that university presidents across the nation have become alarmed at the rate of this escalating drudgery. However, if they are to be successful in controlling the situation, civics as an essential subject must be made compulsory for all university students with immediate activation and built into their courses. The school curriculum must be changed or modified from grade 3 to 12 and beyond in the American system of education. Civics on its own as a subject should be re-introduced into the curriculum from grade 3 to 12 and into the colleges and universitiesof other nations.

President Bush of the United States should be congratulated on his support of "abstinence until marriage" programs for the Americans. The National Center for Health Statistics interviewed teenagers in one-on-one conversation in their homes and found that American teenagers are waiting longer to engage in sexual intercourse. The report validated the program to be going in the right direction, and President Bush has backed the abstinence-only program with $170 million in federal funding in 2005. While the efforts of President Bush are laudable on this program which is aimed at reducing the likelihood of teenage pregnancy and a sexually transmitted disease such as AIDS, it is only the first step in the long journey toward a re-education of the youth and adults of the nation.

The writer believes that if the USA takes the lead in promoting the right type of education in which values such as chastity, honesty, character, morality, and sanctity of life are entrenched in all areas of the curriculum from K1-12 in schools and for all university freshmen, some, if not most, of our problems (alcoholism, drug use, sexual predators) would diminish or disappear. However, this effort in the USA should be emulated by other nations.

We see another wrong type of education in the dose of hatred being given by certain sections or sects of Islam. Probably the bestplace to start the "turn-around" would be in Saudi Arabia. It has been reported that some Saudi militants try to kill or capture only the non-Muslims and let Muslims and Arabs go in terrorist attack. The Associated Press quoted a Lebanese woman, Orora Naoufal, who was taken hostage in her apartment, as saying that the gunmen released her when they learned of her nationality. They told her they were interested in harming only "infidels" and Westerners. It is claimed that the terrorists learned intolerance and discrimination in the Saudi Public School System and religious curriculum. There are many courageous and progressive Saudis who want their country to be more open and tolerant, and it has been reported recently that the Saudi English-language daily Arab news recently published a series by the liberal Saudi writer Raid Qusti about the need to re-evaluate Saudi education. Qusti quoted the editor of Al Riyandh newspaper as saying the people carrying out the latest rash of attacks inside Saudi Arabia have the same ideology as the Saudi extremists who seized the Grand Mosque in Mecca in 1979. They had an ideology of accusing all the others of being "infidels," thereby giving themselves a license to kill them. The editor then remarked that "If we as a nation decline to look at the root causes, as we have for the past two decades, it will only be a matter of time before another group of people with the same ideology springs up." Have we helped create these monsters?" He continues by adding that "Our education system which does not stress tolerance of other faiths, let alone followers of other Islamic schools of thought, is one thing that needs to be re-evaluated from top to bottom. Saudi culture itself and the fact the majority of us do not accept other life-styles and impose our own on other people is another. And the fact that from the fourth to the 12th grade we do not teach our children that these are other civilizations in the world and that we are part of the global community and only stress the Islamic empires over and over is also worth re-evaluating. And last but certainly not least, the religious climate in the country must change."

Hamza Qablan Almozainy, an Arabic professor at King Saud University, published two articles in the Saudi daily Al Watan about "the culture of death in our schools and the role that Saudi teachers are playing in promoting discussions on how bodies are prepared for burial and how the kind of life a person has led — righteous or decadent — can be read from the condition of the person's dead body. This effort to abstain from the attraction of life," he said, "only ends up making some Saudi youth easy targets for extremists trying to recruit young people for Jihad operations. Does the Education Ministry really know about the activities taking place in its schools?" Al-Mozainy asked.

Latest report from Saudi Arabia indicates the government is taking some form of action, and this is highly commendable. There are very good positive teachings in Islam which should be mentioned and counted as the right type of education. One of the most successful and highly commendable is abstinence from alcoholism and smoking. This, in a way, eradicates the problems of alcoholism and smoking which have cost many people their lives. The body is respected, which means respect for the creator of the body. It also means that the body is not abused and, hence, not subjected to various ailments enveloped in alcoholism and smoking.

Another highly successful Islamic teaching is the attire of women which covers the whole body from the head to the feet. The main reason is to prevent men from lusting after their bodies. Exposure of the breasts and beautiful legs of women sends a majority of men to the fantasy world in which every imaginable motive leads them not only to temptations but to various unacceptable behaviors. The enforcement of the women's attire undoubtedly reduces fornication and adultery and, on this tone, has helped the religious aspirations of both men and women of the Islamic faith.

In the Christian faith, God does not force anyone to follow His laws and rules. Right from creation, He gives Adam and Eve freedom to choose. God has the power, authority and right as the Creator of man, to force him into submission, but that is completely at variance with His principles and policies. He is the Author of Freedom who delights in obedience from the heart rather than enslavement and forced submission. When God sent Jesus into the world, Jesus did not force anyone to follow Him or God. He appealed to them. He didnot take away the freedom of the scribes and Pharisees who, in their blindness, bitterly opposed him. When Jesus rose from the dead, He appeared to many people; and before His ascension to Heaven, Hegave the "Great Commission" to His disciples (Matthew 28:19-20), "Go, ye. therefore, and teach all nations, baptizing them in the name of the Father, and of the Son, and of the Holy Spirit, teaching them to observe all things whatsoever I have commanded you, and lo, I am with you always even unto the end of the age."

Love, the most powerful essence that can bring peace, joy, happiness, is the flagship of the Christians, if the instructions of our Master and Savior Jesus are followed. St. Paul, the Great Apostle of Christ, wondered why God, after giving His only son to mankind, did not force man to come to Him but appeal to them through what the Apostle called the "foolishness of preaching" to bring people to God and Christ. This is because God gives us freedom and free will. He wants us, of our own freewill, to be obedient to His ordinances; and, if we are, then we shall reap the benefits of His blessings. If we are disobedient and rebellious to His laws, then we reap the unpalatable consequences of misery, suffering, diseases, and lack of peace. Why? It is because He created the universe with immutable laws that cannot be violated without consequences. It is also the nature of who He is. "With the merciful, He will show Himself merciful; with an upright man, He will show Himself upright; with the pure, He will show Himself pure; and with the rebellious, He will show Himself shrewd" (Psalm 18:25-26). The world has not known the nature of God, and that is why we have problems we should not have. For example, His oracle says, "No good thing will be with-held from those who walk uprightly." The question is Are you walking uprightly? Am I walking uprightly? To answer the question honestly and properly will lead us into the arena of absolute truth. From the foregoing, we have read about the importance of the right type of education in the life of an individual. We have learned that the genotype (genetic constitution) and the environment in which the individual develops play a significant part in the upbringing and education of the individual. We cannot deny the existence of forces acting on the individual. We know that every individual is subject to the forces of gravity and electromagnetism, and we recognize the fact that "As a man thinketh, so he is."

We, therefore, see the importance of the right type of education in the life of a man. The conclusion of this chapter is that the right typeof education begins with the knowledge and fear of God because the foundation of knowledge and the embodiment of all knowledge is God. A good friend of the writer, "Sir" Emmanuel Jiya, wrote about forty years ago, that "Education without the fear and knowledge of God is like space expedition without aeronautical instruments." It is amazing that people have very disturbing interpretations and misconceptions about the knowledge of God, which was confined to religion by man. God is the greatest scientist of all ages, and He wants us to have knowledge in all areas of life including science. It is erroneously believed that religion hampers the advancement of science and knowledge. This is far from the truth. It was men and not God who kept their fellow men down in what has been force-fully described as "man's inhumanity to man." Men used and are using the platform of religion to commit crimes in the name of their God, whom they do not know. This shows that man does not know the God he serves and is doing his own will as usual, contrary to the direction of God as revealed in His Holy Scriptures.

God holds very dearly the life of an individual; hence, when one sinner repents, there is rejoicing in Heaven. Jesus, in his prayer recorded in John 17:25, says, "0 righteous Father, the world hath not known thee." We see that 2,000 years after this memorable declaration, the world still does not know God. An interesting article of an irate journalist supports this truth. Thomas Friedman, in a Times Newspaper article, wrote recently about the desecration of God's creations. "In reaction to an unsubstantiated Newsweek story, Muslims killed sixteen other Muslims in Afghanistan in rioting. Muslims claiming to act in the name of Allah are indiscriminately butchering people without a word of condemnation coining from Muslim leaders. I don't understand a concept of the sacred that says a book is more sacred than a human life. A holy book, whether the Bible or the Koran, is only holy to the extent that it shapes human life and behavior. From what I know of Islam, it teaches that you show reverence to God by showing reverence for His creations, not just His words." Obviously, Mr. Friedman is making a sincere observation on what touched his heart. We see parallels in the time of Jesus when the Pharisees, leaders of the Jewish religion confronted Jesus about keeping the Sabbath Day. Jesus told them that the Sabbath is made for man and not man for the Sabbath. In like manner, the Muslims should be told by their leaders that the Koran is given to guide and shape their lives. It is not, therefore, surprising that God says in the Holy Bible. "These people honor me with their mouths, but their hearts are far from me." What do we make of all this? What is man? Is he an enigma? Let us look at man in the next chapter.

What is Man?

In order to understand life or the meaning of life, it is of para-mount importance that we know who is man or what is man. If we look carefully at the physical appearance of a man or a woman, we are stunned not only by beauty, but also by the structure, features, stature, and composure of this miracle in front of us. What am I? Who am I? Where do I come from? These are questions that cross the mind.

From time immemorial, man has been trying to figure out who he is. David, the Great King of Israel, celebrated warrior, accomplished poet, and prophet of God, asked the same timeless question in Psalm 8. "What is man, that thou art mindful of him, and the son of man, that thou visitest him?" The inference from King David is that God cares for man, hence His visitations to man. Man is a curious being, a trait inherited from his forebears. All the thinkers and philosophers of the ages cannot come up with a satisfying answer. There have been so many theories about man, the beginning of life, and the planet earth in which man lives. In modern times, man is still curious about the beginning of life and the origin of the universe.

In the 19'h century, Charles Darwin proposed the "Theory of Evolution." It was openly accepted and acclaimed and even taught in schools and colleges as if it were a fact and not a mere theory. In the 20th century, the "Big Bang Theory" was proposed. The theory states that the Universe began in a state of compression to infinite density and has been expanding since some particular instant that marked the origin of the universe. The Big Bang is the most generally accepted cosmological theory. Leakey and other scientists gave us the "missing links," while others gave us the "string theory" and various other theories which do not fit and are, therefore, unsatisfactory.

However, Moses, the law giver and prophet of God, authoritatively wrote in Genesis I that "In the beginning, God created the heaven and the earth." What then is man? After many great experiences of life, David said in Psalm 139 about God: "You were the one who fashioned my inward parts, you knitted me together in my mother's womb; you know me through and through when I was formed in secret; woven in the depths of the earth. Your eyes foresaw my deeds, and they were all recorded in your book; my life was fashioned before it had come into being." Let us take a second look at the last phrase. "My life was fashioned before it had come into being" has been corroborated, substantiated and proven true by our scientific knowledge of DNA. We can certainly infer from the above statement that God is the Designer, Builder, Creator, and Sustainer of life of a man or woman. Without any argument, let us read what an eminent scientist writes about the human body. Richard Walker, a biologist, writes in his foreword to The Encyclopedia of the Human Body the following confessions, "My very up-to-date computer pales into insignificance when compared with the miracle of natural engineering that is the human body, the living thing that has always fascinated me as a biologist." The manner in which the body itself, constructed and moved, how it is controlled, how it maintains itself, and how it reproduces and changes during life, coupled with the facts that man functions in both the spiritual realm and the physical world, testifies to the truth that man is the highest manifestation of the Creator God. We see beauty, wisdom, and purpose when we look at a man. From the hair on his head to his feet, every part of the structure is related to its function. The number of hairs on the head is immeasurable. They perform the function of warm bloodedness. The body's internal temperature remains steady at almost exactly 98.4° F (37°C) whatever the conditions outside. To stay at this temperature, the body produces heat at the same rate it loses it. This balancing act is controlled by the hypothalamus. If the blood temperature falls, the hypothalamus kicks in actions that produce more heat and that make it harder for heat to escape. How is the hypothalamus able to do this work efficiently and flawlessly? The writer has great news and revelations for you. Before man invented the television and monitors, God placed various "television monitors" in various places and parts of our bodies. The hypothalamus has a monitor screen that reveals everything going on. The headquarters of the channel is the brain. How great is the Creator and Designer of man! Job, an historical person who lived in the patriarchal period, was among one of the wisest men on earth. He asked in his book Job 7:17, "What is man, that God should magnify him, that God should set His heart upon man and that God should visit him every morning and test him every moment?" Putting together all his experiences of God and life, Job declared in his book Chapter

33:4, "The spirit of God hath made me, and the breath of the almighty hath given me life." What brilliance!

Isaiah, the great Jewish prophet who "saw the Lord sitting upon a throne, high and lifted tip," confirmed in Isaiah 44:2 that God made man, formed him in the womb. This consolidates the truth as science itself confirms the process of formation of the baby in the womb of the mother. It is somewhat axiomatic that man who lives and functions in the visible and invisible world should demand the proof of God's work. A great poet wrote that the "Heavens declare the Glory of God and the firmament shows His handiwork."

If man does not see the heart inside him which pumps blood all around the body for the maintenance and sustenance of life, how does man expect to see God? If you tell a man that he has a brain which controls all his activities, and he argues with you that it is untrue because he cannot see the brain on his head, his unbelief does not alter or change the fact that he has a brain controlling all his activities. The truth is that whether man believes or not, he is a property of God and lives at the expense of God in a world created by God through the Spirit of God who is the universal spirit of all men whether they are black, white, yellow, pink, colored, or other imaginable descriptions. King David of Israel tells us that the parts of the human body are fashioned by God.

Let us now continue our exploratory work of man and the parts of man scientifically and see whether they correspond or match the declaration of Job, Isaiah and King David. Please remember that our investigation is valid if we have man or woman in front of us as a living specimen; but if that is impossible, please get a large mirror in front of you as a substitute for human specimen. We have looked at man, and we have seen the hairs on his head, and we are now going to look at the head of a man to see wonders upon wonders. Embedded in the head are the eyes, the ears, the nose and the mouth but most importantly the brain. While it is not the writer's intention to turn this work into a biology book, it is, however, necessary to mention the salient parts and how they are related to functions showing purpose, wisdom, guidance and direction in every area we look into. Robert Finn in 1983 wrote that "The human brain is the most complex structure in the universe."

This statement itself is a testimony to the fact that man is the highest manifestation of God in creation. Finn goes on to say that the brain has so many interconnections within it that, if it evolved, its evolution, even over billions of years, would be easy to measure. The fact that there is no hint that the brain is evolving is a good argument against evolution. It is calculated that the human brain can store up 100 trillion to 500 trillion bits of information. The most powerful supercomputer of man today cannot equal one percent of this. The human brain contains the largest television station of the body. It can simultaneously order leg muscles to run and the heart to beat faster. The brain gives creativity, memory, intelligence, emotions, and personality. It turns messages received from sensors into sensations that allow us human beings to see, hear, taste, smell and touch. As the Corporate Office of the nervous system, the brain is the control center of the body. Please, dear readers, think of this. There are over 100 billion neurons which sort and sift incoming information at incredible speed and guide the body through an infinite variety of different movements. Random evolution with no director or direction cannot produce this marvel. The brain is divided into three regions.

The forebrain is mainly cerebrum, inside of which are the thalamus and the hypothalamus. The hypothalamus has a monitor that specializes in providing information in the perfection of its work.

The brain stem directly beneath it connects the forebrain to the spinal cord. The cerebellum, which means "little brain," is tucked under the cerebrum behind the brain stem. We see wisdom and a great work of a super scientist when we realize that there are two control systems in the human body, and they work in different ways. Whereas the nervous system uses electrical signals to make cells respond, the endocrine system uses chemical messengers called hormones that are released into the blood. Hormones are produced by endocrine glands which empty directly into the blood stream. Three major endocrine glands including the pituitary gland are in the head. The hypothalamus produces some hormones and forms the main link between the nervous system and the endocrine system. The pituitary gland is the orchestra of the endocrine system. It produces various hormones and controls many other endocrine glands. It is the control center of the endocrine system. The pineal gland is connected to nerves from the eyes and controls body rhythms such as sleeping and waking. Here we see the wisdom of the Maker of Man. Before man discovered electricity, God the Creator put electrical signals in the human body, showing us again that the science of man is ages behind the science of God. Mapping the body shows design and wisdom of a super scientist. Each spinal nerve supplies a particular part of the body, including an area of skin. Is this not a marvel? Remember, we are still investigating man from the head, and we have read about the brain and spinal cord in the head. Now, let us look at the eyes embedded in the head.

Let us look at the visible part of the structure and how it is related to function:

1) Our eyelids protect the eyes from bright light and foreign objects; when we blink, they wipe the eyes and keep them clear of dust.

2) Our eyelashes stop too much light from entering the eyes as well as protect the eyes from foreign particles.

3) Our eyebrows direct sweat away from the eyes and help keep out some light.

4) Our tear ducts empty tears onto the surface of the eye.

5) The tear glands are tinder the outer edge of the eyebrows and produce tears.

Here, again, we see wisdom of the Maker because there is a purpose for each structure. Let us now look at the invisible part, the part that is inside the head. Before we do this, let us remember the declaration of the Lord Jesus Christ about the eye. He said that the eye is the light of the body; and, from our study of the human body, we know that vision is the foremost of the special senses.

The eye in an adult measures 2.5 cm across and contains 125 million photo-receptors or light visible cells inside the eye. The eyeball is divided into two unequal chambers on either side of the lens. The rear chamber which makes up most of the eye is filled with a transparent, jelly-like substance called vitreous humor. Vitreous humor gives the eye its shape and keeps the retina in position. The front of the eye is filled with aqueous humor, a clear fluid between the lens and the cornea that keeps the cornea curved outward. The lens is made of layers of crystal-clear proteins. It changes the shape to focus incoming light.

The ciliary muscles form a ring of muscle that focuses light by changing the shape of the lens. Humans have binocular vision because their eyes face forward. You cannot study the structure and functions of each part of the eye and not burst into a song of praise to the Highest God for His wisdom. Evolution is just out of the question. It does not and cannot measure up to standard.

Let us look at our ears. The ear is the organ responsible for sending both auditory information and space orientation information to the brain. Our ears consist of three parts: the external ear, which receives the sound waves; the middle ear, which transmits the vibrations by a series of three small bones (hammer, anvil, and stapes); and the inner or internal ear, a complex bony chamber placed deep in the skull. Fluid inside a narrow tube, the cochlea, vibrates. These vibrations stimulate tiny hairs on nerves. These nerves send electrical impulses to the brain, which enables us to recognize the sound. Therefore, the molecular machinery and complex systems in the cell depend upon far too many interconnected parts to have been built up gradually tiny step by tiny step over time. Removal of one part of the system causes the part to stop functioning.

There are other cogent points against the Theory of Evolution:

1) Self-replicating life by random chance is extremely unlikely because it clashes with the "cell theory."

2) Life appeared too quickly for random chance. Scientists tell us that earth and the solar system were formed about 4-5 billion years ago. Until 5 billion years ago, the earth was too hot and was totally unfit for any kind of life. According to the scientists, earth suffered impacts from giant asteroids until about 3.9 billion years ago. In rock 3.86 billion years old is found tars and graphite produced by biological activity. Bacteria are found in rocks 3.5 billion years old. The conclusion is that life appeared very soon (150 million years) after life was possible and much too soon to be accounted for by natural means. This earliest step in evolution is very much in disarray.

3) Evolution suggests smooth changes and transitions from one species to another (called "gradualism") which is not found in the fossil record.

4) *"Punctuated Equilibrium" produces unfitness for survival.*

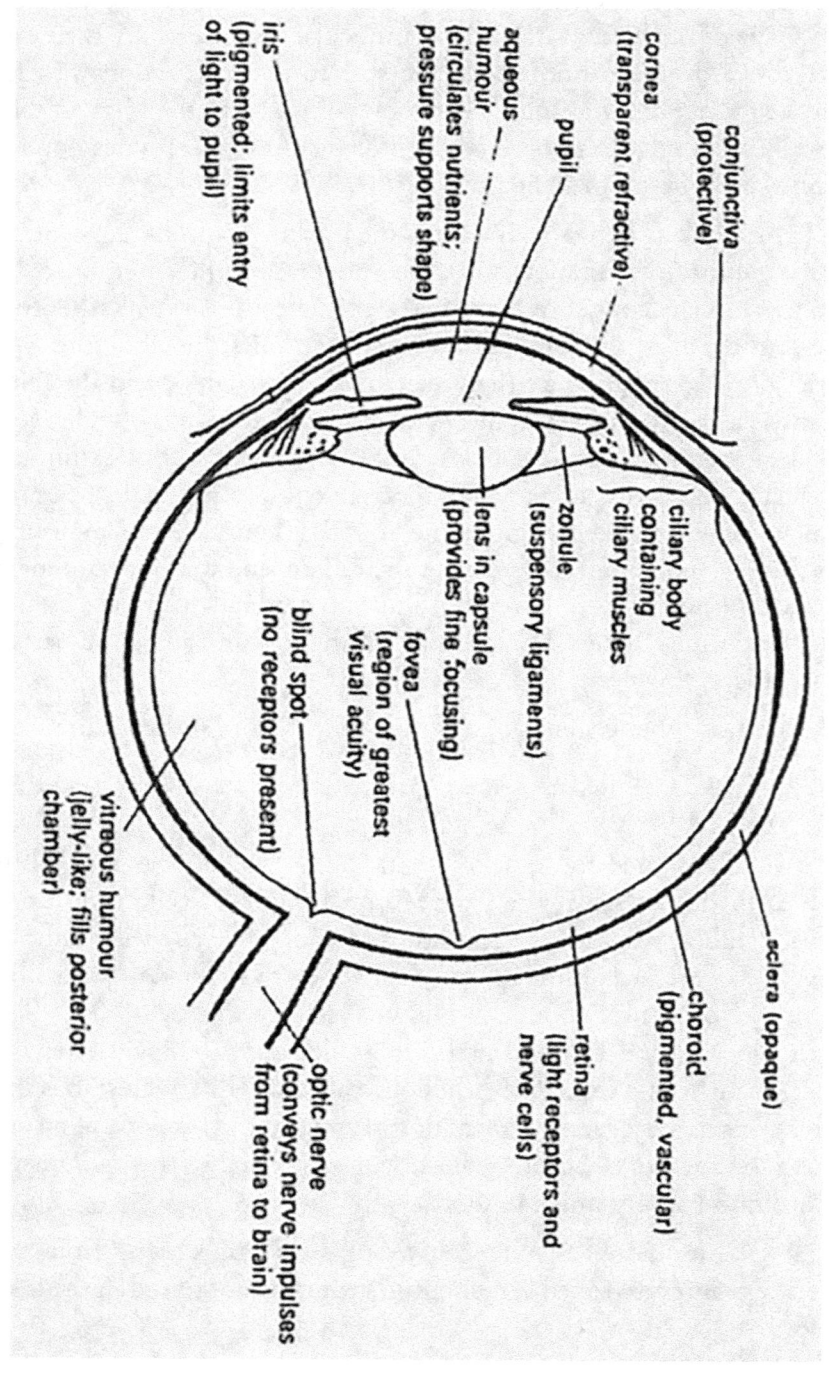

conjunctiva
(protective)

cornea
(transparent refractive)

pupil

aqueous
humour
(circulates nutrients;
pressure supports shape)

iris
(pigmented; limits entry
of light to pupil)

ciliary body
containing
ciliary muscles

zonule
(suspensory ligaments)

lens in capsule
(provides fine focusing)

fovea
(region of greatest
visual acuity)

blind spot
(no receptors present)

vitreous humour
(jelly-like; fills posterior
chamber)

sclera (opaque)

choroid
(pigmented, vascular)

retina
(light receptors and
nerve cells)

optic nerve
(conveys nerve impulses
from retina to brain)

5) Evolution says that changes are by random chance and, therefore, are not repeatable; yet nature has similar organisms that are unrelated.

6) Convergence is the tendency of unrelated organisms to have nearly identical anatomical and physiological characteristics; convergence runs counter to evolutionary theory.

7) Scientists tell us that Cambrian "explosion" occurred 540 million years ago and, in a few years, produced nearly all the animal phyla (same architectural design) ever to exist (70+). There have been no new phyla since. Skeletons appeared. Out of 182 possible skeletal designs, 146 showed up at this time. Creatures that evolutionists thought appeared sequentially emerged at the same time.

8) Evolutionists have not been able to show an evolutionary pathway (pylogeny) for humans. The pathways constructed morphologically (cranial and dental features) and molecularly (gene and protein sequences) do not coincide.

9) Y-chromosome sequences demonstrate recent origin for humans.

10) DNA language shows intelligence. DNA is a language or code made up of four letters. Four different compounds (bases) are used for the letters. The letters give a message that is independent of the chemistry (type of compounds used). The sequencing of the letters provides the message/information.

The proponents of the Theory of Evolution appear to concentrate on evolution of man. If evolution were true and man evolved from primordial or pre-biotic soup when pre-biotic reacted to form amino acids, sugars, and fatty acids, when then did a woman evolve to have beautiful facial features, superb breast with figure, head-raising backside that always sends men to the crazy house? When we look at the biological differences, the mental attitude and thinking of a woman contrasted with that of a man, the Theory of Evolution collapses and crumbles to pieces.

The recent exhibition of "Bodies" in Tampa, Florida, by MOSI from August 2005, has done a great service to education. It is a consolidation of this chapter in visual form. Dr. Roy Glover, Chief Medical Adviser for "Bodies — the Exhibition" contends that the primary goal of the exhibition is education, to help both children and adults better understand the mysteries and the wonders that lie beneath their skin. It is important that people know about their bodies and the effect that disease has on them and are challenged to make better health care choices. One fact any open-minded visitor to that exhibition admits is that Intelligent Design stares tantalizingly at us all. There has been so much controversy about Intelligent Design, and some of its backers have been accused of promoting religion under the guise of science. But after looking at "Bodies — the Exhibition" at MOSI which gives us all "the opportunity to explore the wonders of the human body especially the inner workings of our bodies in a way that we never have before," it is a denial of science to argue against Intelligent Design of man. If the definition of science (from the Latin words "scio," "scire," is "what we know," the "Bodies" exhibition shows us that seeing is believing; and Intelligent Design of man speaks loud and clear to viewers, in silence. It is not an argument about religion or science. It is about what we learn from what we see. This is the right type of education which the author advocates. The right type of education will lead us to the absolute truth without any stress, argument, ideological, or religious beliefs.

The Iowa State University molecular biologist Thomas Ingebritsen has used mouse traps in his seminar class on "God and Science" to teach "irreducible Complexity." Other notable scientists like Professors Belte, Johnson, Dembski, and others have stated that the cell is "irreducibly complex" and, therefore, the Theory of Evolution is flawed.

The fact and conclusion of the matter is that we cannot argue against the truth that the

"Bodies" exhibition advertises and proclaims Intelligent Design in man, and this can be extended to all plants and animals. The way land plants absorb water from the soil through their roots and send it through their stems like a pipe to the leaves shows intelligent design and wisdom.

Teaching the truth of what we see and know is not advocacy of religion or creationism but a realization of the truth.

THE HUMAN EAR

A close look at the Human ear, completely destroys the theory of evolution, but advertises the wisdom of the Maker in the design and pattern of the structure and function of each part of the ear.

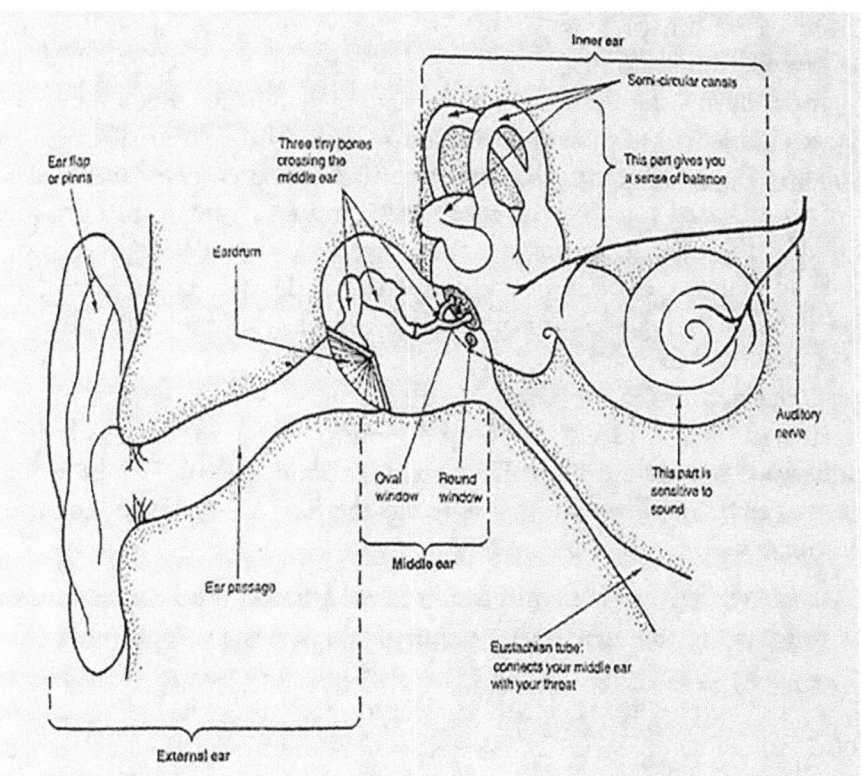

The Creator and Maker of Man is a Super Designer as seen in the above diagram where complex organ of the ear which shows complexity of structure is conspicuously seen.

Let us continue our investigation of man, remembering that we are still on the visible and invisible parts of the head. We have briefly covered the eyes and ears embedded in the head, and now we shall look at the mouth and the nose. Inside our mouth are the teeth, and they are the hardest objects in the body. Teeth cut, crush and chew the food that we eat, making it easier to both swallow and digest. There are differences between teeth. The incisors at the front are the only teeth that have a flat cross-section. I hope you are sitting or standing in front of the mirror as you read this. Please open your mouth in front of the mirror to confirm what you are reading. You will see that the incisors have a flat cross-section with a single cutting edge. They take large chunks out of food and slice it up. The canines have a single point for gripping and tearing. Behind them are the premolars and molars which are used for chewing food and grinding it down into a paste. If we look at the structure of a tooth, we are overawed. Tooth enamel is made almost entirely of rod-shaped crystals of calcium phosphate packed tightly together. It is not only the hardest substance in the body but also the heaviest with extremely high resistance to wear and tear. See the wonder of the Creator! Enamel does not contain cells, and it does not need a blood supply. A tooth's framework is made of a substance called dentine which resembles bone. Dentine supports the tooth's enamel crown, and it also forms the roots that anchor the tooth in the jaw.

Dear readers, we are still inside the mouth and the next important wonder is the tongue. In the tongue, we have taste receptors that are clustered together in "taste buds" which line the sides of the tongue's "bumps" or papillae. Each taste receptor ends in a short filament or taste hair which protrudes into taste bud's outer pore. The hairs detect chemicals dissolved in food and drink and send signals along nerves to the brain. What a beauty! The tongue also contains receptors for temperature and pain sensors. Praise be to the scientist of the ages.

So far, our scientific explorations show perfection, purpose, guidance, direction and specialization of the materials in the head. It has been said that smell and taste are mutual partners and work in identical way. Both are chemical senses; taste detects substances that are dissolved in saliva, while smell detects those present in the air. In order to do this, they use chemo receptors, which are specialized cells that respond to specific molecules. While we are pondering the wisdom of the director of all those processes, let us look at the respiratory system of man. The respiratory system consists of the lungs and the airways — nose, pharynx (throat), larynx (voice box), trachea (wind pipe) and bronchi — that carry air between the lungs and the outside atmosphere.

As we are about to leave the head and move down to the chest cavity and the stomach area, we see fantastic integration and synchronization between the head and other parts of the body. We see this in the respiratory system just mentioned. Whereas the body can do without food and water for a short time, it cannot survive without a continuous supply of oxygen. Its trillions of cells constantly consume oxygen to release energy from sugars to provide power for their activities.

As we move away from the head into the chest cavity and the abdominal cavity (stomach area), we are confronted with the stark reality of the fact that man lives in both the visible and the invisible world. We can only see our chest cavity and abdominal cavity physically, but inside the chest and the abdominal cavity are the existence of organs we cannot see with our naked eyes. However, we know they are there because medical doctors and other professional scientists have opened up the body several times and photographed the internal area which we cannot see with our naked eyes. My friends and dear readers, if we cannot see the lungs and the heart within us, how do we expect to see God who is invisible? Let us briefly go through the process of breathing. As we breathe in air, it travels along the nose, pharynx, larynx and trachea, before entering one of two branches — the bronchi inside the lungs, bronchi divide into smaller and smaller branches that finally end in pouch-like alveoli where oxygen and carbon dioxide are exchanged. Let us consider the larynx or voice box which links the pharynx and trachea. It is constructed from a framework of cartilage pieces, including the thyroid cartilage whose prominence, the Adam's apple can be felt midway down the front of the neck.

THE HUMAN RESPIRATORY SYSTEM

A close look at the Human Respiratory system completely rules out evolution, but shows wisdom and Design, in an area where the superlative wisdom of the Maker is magnificently seen with the arrangement of all the structures of the lungs, heart, diaphragm and the ribs.

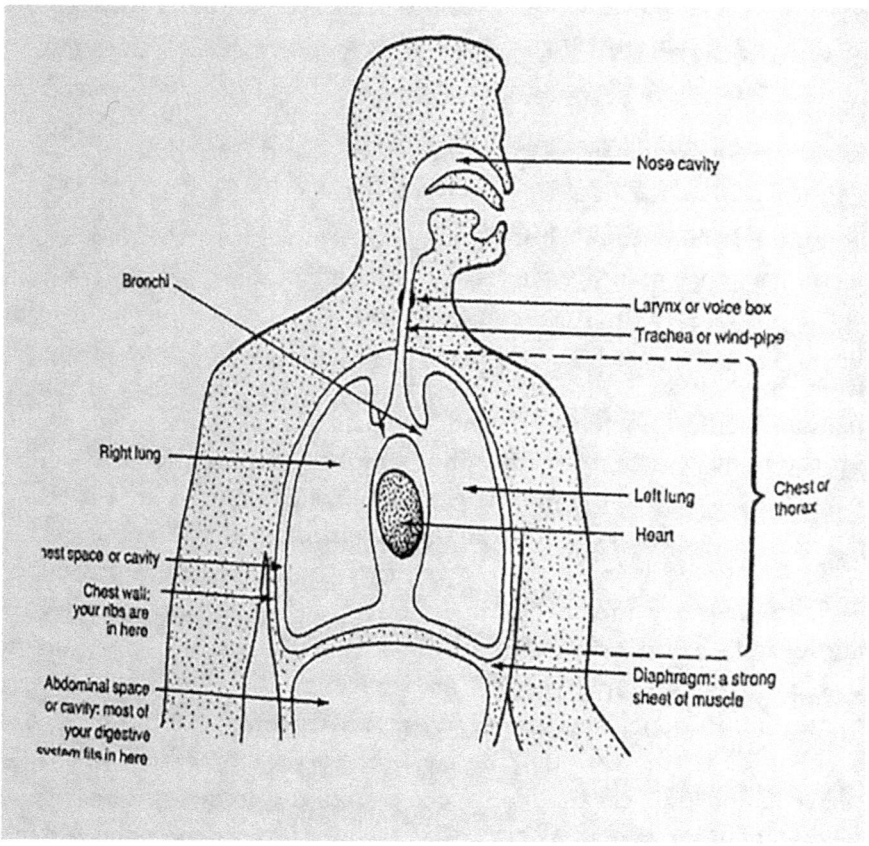

The Creator and Maker of Man is a Super Designer as seen in the above diagram where complex organs of the heart and lungs are superbly inserted in the chest area. The rib cage shows the wisdom of the designer.

The larynx has two main roles. First, "as guardian of the airways," it ensures that air normally has free passage to and from the lungs but closes off the airway using the epiglottis when food is being swallowed. The epiglottis is hinge-like and stands upright, clear of the opening of the larynx. This is the normal position of the epiglottis, and it allows air to pass freely through the larynx. The epiglottis alone can be used as an argument against evolution. If evolution process has no purposeful input, no creator, no director, then the larynx (voice box) destroys that argument because it closes off the airways using epiglottis when food is being swallowed. There is, therefore, a director of operations of all the activities going on the body. Having looked at the airways, let us now glimpse at the lungs. The lungs are light spongy structures that are approximately conical in shape. Each lung is divided into separate portions called lobes. The right lung consists of three lobes, whereas the left lung, which is slightly smaller in order to make space for the heart, consists of two lobes. Here, again, we see the wisdom of the designer of the chest area. The rib cage protects the lungs, and its muscles assist in breathing. The two lungs contain about 300 million alveoli that collectively provide a surface area for gas exchange of 750 square feet, thirty-five times the surface area of the skin, squeezed into a space inside the chest that is no bigger than a shopping bag. Is this not a wonder in itself? Imagine how excited the Italian Physiologist Lazzaro Spallanzani (1729-99) was when he proved that cell respiration occurs in every tissue of the body.

May I please have your attention again? We are still in the chest area, and we have just finished with the lungs, but we move to look at the heart which is in a lubricated sac called pericardium in the left center of the chest (thorax). The structure and function of the heart are awesome. In the adult human body, the heart beats about 70 times per minute or approximately 100,000 beats per day. During exercise or intense emotion, the human heart rate can increase to 200 beats per minute. Thus, in a life span of seventy-five years, with everyday stresses and emotions, a human heart may beat more than three billion times.

The heart is one of the most efficient natural pumps men has known. The heart pumps approximately 100 milliliters of the blood per beat. In seventy-five years, this amounts to 300 million liters of blood. Our heart consists of two pumps. The right side of the heart pumps blood to the lungs where the blood is oxygenated and then returns to the heart. This circuit is called the pulmonary circulation. The left side of the heart receives oxygenated blood from the lungs and pumps it to the rest of the body. The circuit of blood from the left side of the heart to the periphery and then back to the heart is called the systemic circulation.

No one can argue against the truth and fact that "blood is life." When the writer was growing up as a young boy, he saw how people took live chickens and slaughtered them. As soon as the animal lost an appreciable amount of blood, it died. That confirms to the writer from a tender age that "blood is life." Blood supplies the needs of the body's trillion of cells, ensuring that they are kept in safe, constant surroundings. It does this demanding role in three ways! First, it acts as the body's delivery and collection service, carrying blood, oxygen, hormones, and other essentials to cells, and removing wastes. Second, it distributes heat evenly around the body, keeping cells at a steady 98.4°F (37°C). Third, it helps defend the body against infection. This shows the wisdom of God and destroys the theory of random evolution.

My dear readers, please think of this for a moment, in a single drop of blood, there are approximately 250 million red blood cells, 16 million platelets, and 375,000 white blood cells. Red blood cells also known as erythrocytes, are produced at the rate of 2 million per second in the red marrow of certain bones. How great is the wisdom of the Creator and Designer of man! Red blood cells carry oxygen to the tissues and also transport some of the carbon dioxide produced as a waste product by the cells of the body. Red blood cells in the body do not have nuclei. White blood cells of different types detect and destroy invading disease, causing microorganisms. Blood platelets stop leaks from blood vessels by making blood clot.

The Bombshell: In Every Human, the Mark of Jesus, the Creator

Dear readers, get ready to read the bombshell that destroys the theory of evolution. Paul tells us in his Epistle to the Colossians.

THE CODE OF OWNERSHIP:

THE FIGURE 8 DOUBLE CIRCULATION OF BLOOD IN EVERY HUMAN BEING: THE SIGN, MARK, AND STAMP OF THE CREATOR: THE DIVINE NUMBER OF JESUS IN EVERY HUMAN.

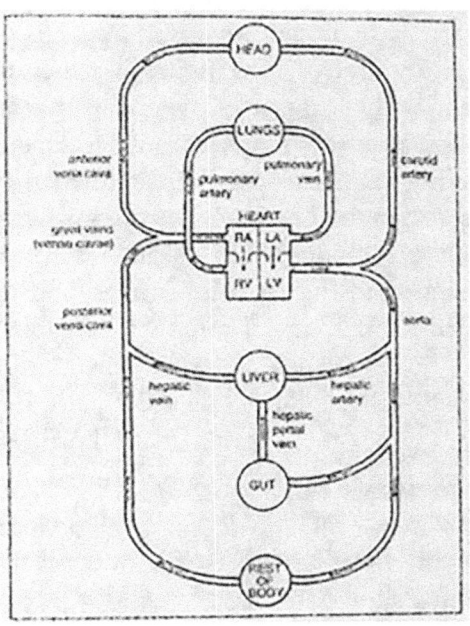

THIS IS WHY 'EVERY KNEE SHALL BOW AND CONFESS THAT JESUS IS LORD OF ALL.'

Chapter 1:16, "For by Jesus Christ were all things created, that are in Heaven, and that are in earth, visible and invisible, whether they be thrones, or dominions or principalities or powers, all things were created by Him and for Him." Verse 17 says Jesus is before all things, and by Him all things exist.

The bombshell is that the mark of the Lord Jesus Christ is in every human being. He is the life in every human being. Bearing in mind that "blood is life," Jesus is the Life-giver, and His mark is found in the blood circulatory system. The figure 8 structure of the human circulatory system is the Code of Ownership of man by Jesus, and that is why the scripture says that "Every knee shall bow and confess that He is the Lord." It is through Him that man is created. Inside the human body is a system of blood carrying tubes that if stretched out would extend over 93,000 miles (150,000 Km.), the equivalent of being wrapped around the earth four times; and some 98% of this incredible distance is made up of microscopic capillaries that ramify every part of the body's tissues. Arteries, veins, and capillaries, form a circulation network that follows a figure 8 path, the divine number of the Lord Jesus Christ, the imprint of the Lord Jesus Christ as the authentic sole owner, and creator of every human being without any exemption, and that is why on His return to the earth, every knee shall bow and confess that He is the Lord — because his mark is on all creations.

Why is it that at this time it has pleased God in His mercies for this revelation? The answer is simple. It is not the wish of God that any should perish, but the "Days of Grace" are drawing to a close; and this revelation is meant to draw all people to go through Jesus Christ because "There is no salvation in any other, and there is no other name under Heaven given among men, whereby we must be saved." Dear reader, you can find out the truth yourself and confirm for yourself this statement which may appear stupendous to you. Dear readers, you will observe that everyday experience of life confirms that things around us are made by us. The car you drive is probably made by Ford, Honda, Dodge, Lincoln, Volkswagen, Mercedes, Lexus, etc. No piece of iron lying outside you suddenly started evolving from a piece of iron into four tires, car body and, hey, presto a car. A car does not evolve. It was built by manufacturers.

THE HUMAN HEAD

Examination of the Human Head shows wisdom and Design, an area where the brain, the eyes, the ears, the nose, the mouth are housed.

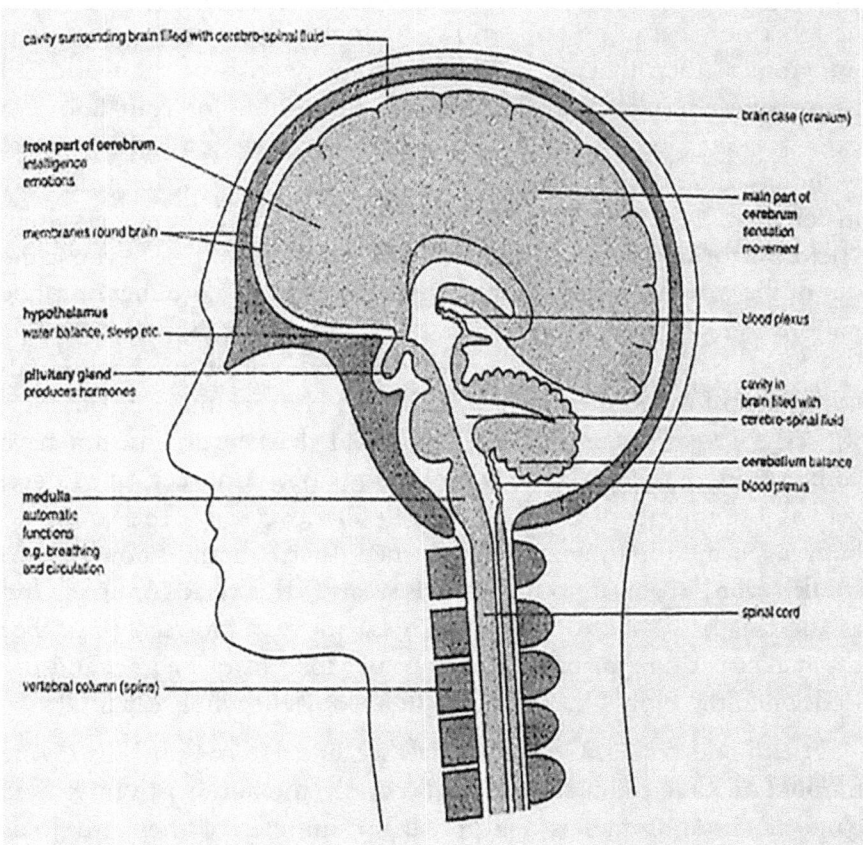

The Creator and Maker of Man is a Super Designer as seen in the above diagram where complex organs of the eyes, the ears, nose, tongue and skin are compacted in an area incredibly small.

In like manner, the house that you live in was designed initially by an architect or a civil engineer, and builders built it according to the plan of the house. It may have five bedrooms, a dining area, three baths, a kitchen; and all the beautiful decorations you have in your house are put there by you. The house did not just evolve from sand, put itself up from dust or sand and go through random changes, with no designer no creator, no builder. Even a fool will not believe that. Is it not ironical then that the so-called clever scientists of the world tell us to believe that man evolved? If it is impossible for your house to exist without a builder or designer, it is impossible for a man to exist without a designer or builder. Listen to what the Holy Scriptures say in Jeremiah 1-5, "Then the word of the Lord came unto me saying: 'Before I formed you in the womb, I knew you, and before you came out of the womb, I sanctified you and ordained you a prophet unto the nations.' God formed Jeremiah in the womb of his mother before he was born. Isaiah, the fearless prophet of God, said in his book Isaiah 49:5, "God formed me in the womb to be His servant." The question was asked: Can a woman forget her child that she should not have compassion on the son of her womb? God says, "Yea, they may forget, yet will I not forget thee." Also in Isaiah 50:4, we read, "The Lord God hath given me the tongue of the learned, that I should know how to speak a word in season to him who is weary." This verse confirms God as the creator of the tongue, and in Isaiah 54:5, we read this: "For thy maker is thine husband, the Lord of Hosts in His name; and thy Redeemer, the Holy One of Israel, the God of the whole earth."

Friend and reader, God is our Maker, and He has put His divine number on us to claim ownership. Secondly, the number twenty-three pairs of chromosomes is another divine number of the Lord Jesus Christ. Two plus three equals five. The number five signifies the five wounds of Christ on the cross at Calvary. This is knowledge St. Paul knew when he wrote that "Christ was slain before the Foundation of the World." In his Epistle to the Ephesians Chapter 1:3-4, he wrote, "Blessed be the God and Father of our Lord Jesus Christ, who hath blessed us with all spiritual blessings in heavenly places in Christ. According as He hath chosen us before the foundation of the world, that we should be Holy and without blame before Him in love." Before the foundation of the world, before man was created, the Lord Jesus was slain to redeem man; and because of this, His divine code and numbers 2 and 3 which equals 5 wounds of redemption of man is in the 23 pairs of chromosomes in every man and woman. The divine numbers 2 and 3 are very significant in the 23 pairs of chromosomes. Here, the divine number 2 stands for God the Father and Jesus His only Begotten son. We see the explanation in Proverbs 8:22-36 when Jesus said, "God possessed him in the beginning of his way, before his works of old."

Verse 23: I was set tip from everlasting, from the beginning, or ever the earth was.

Verse 24: When there were no depths, I was brought forth, when there were no fountains abounding with water.

Verse 25: Before the mountains were settled, before the hills, was I brought forth!

Verse 26: While as yet he had not made the earth, nor the fields, nor the highest part of the dust of the world

Verse 27: When He prepared the heavens, I was there, when He set a compass upon the face of the depth

Verse 28: When He established the clouds above, when He strengthened the fountains of the deep

Verse 29: When He gave to the sea its decree, that the waters should not pass His commandment; when He appointed the foundations of the earth

Verse 30: Then I was by him, as one brought up with Him, and I was daily His delight, rejoicing always before Him.

This agrees with what St. John the beloved apostle wrote in the Gospel according to St. John 1:1, "In the beginning was the Word, and the Word was with God and the Word was God."

The divine number 3 signifies Father, Son and Spirit. The Spirit is extremely important because it is by the Spirit that our redemption is sealed. So, the number twenty-three echoes the completeness of Father, Son, and Spirit in every human being because every human being is redeemable by the blood of Jesus and sealed unto eternity. Thirdly, because life is in the blood, and the Lord Jesus is the life-giver, the human blood circulation follows the figure eight pattern signifying the divine number of life. This knowledge has been hidden for ages, but praise to God that it is now being revealed to all people of the world so that they may know that Jesus is the "water-shed" of history, and God the Father does not want any to perish because the "Days of Grace" are drawing to a close. Therefore, the message of "repentance" is being repeated and repeated again and again. The message has not changed — "Let the wicked forsake his way, and the unrighteous man his thoughts, and let him return into the Lord, and He will have mercy upon him and to our God, for He will abundantly pardon" (Isaiah 55:7).

"For my thoughts are not your thoughts, neither are your ways my ways, saith the Lord" (Isaiah 55:8).

"For as the heavens are higher than the earth, so are my ways higher than your ways, and my thoughts than your thoughts" (Isaiah 55:9).

It is virtually impossible for the wicked to forsake his way without the help and assistance of the Lord Jesus Christ. This is where the concept of the "new birth" comes in. This is why Lord Jesus told Nicodemus that it is imperative for man to be "born again." Every human being has inherited the genes of sin, rebellion, and condemnation from Adam and Eve. Adam sold himself into the slavery of the devil, hence every man is under the condemnation of sin because the genes of Adam and Eve have been passed on to all human beings. Therefore, in order to keep man under his stronghold, Satan the devil has put doubts in the hearts of men. It is Satan the evil one who has been working in the minds and hearts of the people to deceive them in many ways. People easily hold fast to deceit.

Jeremiah wrote that "Everyone dealt falsely from the prophet even unto the priest. They bend their tongues for lies and are not valiant for the truth upon the earth; for they proceed from evil to evil and do not know God." We do not seem to be different in our actions from the people in the days of Jeremiah. These days, we teach our tongues to speak lies and weary ourselves to commit iniquity. It seems that our habitation is in the midst of deceit, and we refuse to know God. Why? We are deceived because the genes of disobedience, rebellion against God, excessive love of pleasures, are in the hearts and minds of every human being, kept captive by Satan the evil one. Therefore, we have deceptions almost in all walks of life. The advocates of the "Theory of Evolution" tell us there is no God, no Maker, no designer of man, but man evolved from dust and through random changes evolved into a man. The facts of science tell us that evolution is not true, yet it is taught in schools and colleges as if it were a fact and not a theory. Our everyday experience tells us that the house we live in has a builder. The plumbers put in water, bath, sink; the electricians put in wires which produce electricity. We buy our cooking and washing appliances, put in beautiful furniture according to our taste. The house did not evolve from dust. Our body is like a house, and it is built and designed by a maker; but because of the deception of the devil, some people refuse to acknowledge God.

The genes of disobedience, rebellion, desire to do our own will, have been passed on to us by Adam and Eve, and they are located in the hearts and minds of men. That is why nobody teaches a baby to be disobedient or rebellious or to have the desire to do his or her own will. As a parent, think of all the hassles you go through with your children when they are toddlers. They are disobedient and rebellious and want to do their own will. When they grow up to be youths, they think they are wiser than their parents; and they are disobedient, rebellious and bigheaded. Parents who spared the rod when their young ones were still tender, all come to grief and sorrow in life. Have you ever wondered why parents have to go through various difficulties to bring up their children? One of the eternal principles of God that mankind does not yet realize is this — our children do not obey us because we do not obey God our Heavenly Father, and hence we ourselves violate one of the hidden eternals principles of God that has not been expounded to us. This is why God the heavenly Father gave us the commandment that "We must honor our fathers and our mothers" for longevity of life. Our fathers and mothers are not limited to our blood related parents alone, but to all our seniors and elders everywhere in the world because all mankind have a common ancestry in Adam and Eve.

As it grieves our hearts when our children are disobedient and rebellious in following our guide lines, so does the heart of God grieve because we are disobedient and rebellious to Him, our only source of peace, health, happiness, eternal joy and everlasting life. In many cases, the writer has seen disobedient children who beat up their mothers; and in tears, all those mothers said the same words, "Your children will do the same to you." What those mothers did not know was that they were invoking one of the eternal laws of God, enshrined in one of The Ten Commandments; and of all the cases that the writer knows, the "curse" (if you want to put it bluntly) came to pass. Their own children beat them up, too. Every unrighteous act they did to their parents was reciprocated to them; and the cycle goes on. These are facts that as human beings we cannot deny or sweep under the rug, and it is time we look for a solution.

The Race Card: Hot News
Truth? Myth? Latest Scientific Discovery

The rejection of the truth of God by man does not alter the truth of God that He created man. It is the rebellion of man originating from the genes of Adam that man refuses to acknowledge God as the Creator of life, the Sustainer and Preserver of Life. In the so-called "Age of Reason," man tends to be blind and unreceptive to reason and the science he venerates so much. We have seen, and we see daily, the ugly repercussions of one of the most devastating deceptions of the devil —The Race Card.

According to history, white men generally have oppressed black men for centuries and the various reasons given were fabricated in lies, rooted in deceit, watered with salacious propaganda, and bloomed with arrogance serrated with selfishness. So many myths and teachings of men went into circulation. One of the most acceptable in certain parts of the world is that the white man is one of the fallen angels and this view has been supported with the account found in Genesis 6. But there are differing views and interpretations of Genesis 6. According to Genesis 6:2 — "the sons of God" saw the "daughters of men" that they were fair, and they took them wives of all whom they chose." The 1967 edition of the Scofield Reference Bible states that some hold that the "sons of God" were fallen angels "who kept not their first estate" (Jude 6-7). The intrusion into the human sphere consequently produced a race of wicked giants (Genesis 6:46). However, others hold the view that since angels are spoken of in a sexless way (Matt: 22:30) and that the words "took them wives" signifies a lasting marriage, reference has to do with the breakdown of the separation of the godly line of Seth by intermarriage with the godless line of Cain. There has been a refinement of the latter view which indicates that the "sons of God" apply to all the godly, and the "daughters of men" to all the ungodly irrespective of their natural paternity. The salient point here is that whichever view is held, it is obvious that Satan the Devil attempted to corrupt the race that the Messiah could not come to redeem men. But God salvaged a remnant (Genesis 6:8), and a godly line was preserved. The tactics, deceit, falsehood and manipulations of the devil have not changed but have been refined from age to age to suit the prevailing circumstances. The devil (who is a fallen angel and a spirit that can transform himself) has always entered the hearts of unbelieving people and used them to distort, distract, change the truth of God into a lie backed up with phony and misleading or fabricated data to create chaos and confuse the innocents and the unwary.

Destruction of the Race Card? Hot News

The Race Card is one of the deadliest and most potent weapons used daily by the devil to create hatred among men. All over the world, the devil uses the race card and tribal origination to fan hatred between one tribe and another tribe, between black and white, between yellow-skinned and brown-colored skin; and because of the fallen nature of man, he embraces lies quickly and acclaims falsehood with open hands and alacrity. Man's inhumanity to man in every culture and every age is an open secret. All these sufferings happened because of the rejection of the Truth of God by man who wants to do his own will at all times. The devil inflicts spiritual blindness on men and women of every culture, creed, and race so that the cataracts in their eyes do not allow them to see the light of the Truth of God in the face of Jesus Christ.

However, it appears that the race card is about to fall down, and the backbone of racial prejudice is breaking down into pieces as a result of the latest scientific discovery released in December 2005. The discovery lifts the veil on our skin tones. According to Knight Rider Newspaper's report published in *St. Petersburg Times* on Sunday, December 18, 2005, the team of 25 geneticists, molecular biologists and anthropologists, most from Pennsylvania State University, found that the merest fragment of one gene plays a major role in the differing skin colors of black and white people. This means that Caucasians' skin color is the result of a mutated gene according to the experts, "so a significant part of the difference we perceive between the races is caused by just one rung on the twisted ladder of our DNA." Otherwise, as geneticists have been discovering more and more as they study the human genome, we are all pretty much alike. What? Say that again! Is that not what the Holy Bible has been telling us from the beginning, over 3,000 years ago and we refuse to accept and believe? From the latest findings of the scientists, we should admit that God's word as contained in the Holy Bible is true from the beginning. Scientists found that "there's more variation within racial populations than there is between." Theodore Schurr, a University of Pennsylvania anthropologist, said the findings were significant. The research work suggests that the skin-whitening mutation occurred by chance (spiritually questionable as there is nothing called "chance" in the spiritual world) in a single individual, after the first human exodus from Africa, where all people were brown-skinned. That person's offspring apparently thrived as humans moved northward into what is now Europe, helping to give rise to the lightest of the world's races.

Let us for a moment ponder upon two significant facts indirectly presented to us by the findings of the scientists. The first inference and fact is that all authorities, scientists et al, now agree and admit that the first man was from Africa. The second significant fact is that mankind was ONE and is ONE. This amplifies, consolidates, and entrenches the truth of the declaration of the Lord Jesus Christ that all men are brothers, a fact and an ideology later expounded to us by St. Paul that God has made of one blood all nations of the earth according to the Scriptures. If the world had accepted the Word of God now proven to be true by the scientists, would the world have gone through the First World War, or the Second World War? Could the holocaust not have been avoided? Could the murder of hundreds or thousands of black men by the Klu Klux Klan have happened? Could injustice, poverty, and the division of the rich and the poor be avoided knowing that mankind is one and all are brothers and sisters? In certain circles, it is believed that the first man Adam was a black or brown-skinned man, and there is speculation that the Garden of Eden may have been located somewhere in the Northernmost part of Africa towards the east. It is believed that one of the reasons for this speculation is the portion of the Word of God which says, "Out of Egypt (Africa) have I called out my son." The view for this is that the first Adam was an African, and the second Adam, the Lord Jesus Christ, was "called out of Egypt (Africa)." This led to the view by some that the Lord Jesus Christ was black and that the white man twisted facts and history to make Jesus a white man. May I say categorically and emphatically that such a view is erroneous. In the wisdom of God, He already provided the answer before the coming of His Son. In order that the Work of Redemption of man might be complete for all mankind, the Lord Jesus Christ is a combination of black and white-skinned colors. He is the Savior of the white people, of the black people, of the brown-skinned, yellow-skinned and any imaginable skin colors known to man. In short, He is the Savior of mankind, because mankind is one, and mankind has one destiny. All will appear before the throne of God on Judgment Day. My friend, my reader, my brother, my sister, it is time to examine the truth, ponder on the truth, and make your choice. Since the dawn of history, mankind has accepted the existence of many kings, many gods, many lords, many faiths, many spirits; but to Christians, there is one God, one Lord, one Spirit, one faith, one baptism, one mankind (all are brothers and sisters) and one destiny (all will appear before the judgment seat to give an account of their activities and receive rewards).

In the light of the daily discoveries of the scientists validating eternal truths of God, would you not reassess your stand and position? Listen to the latest scientific work now going on in Cambridge, Great Britain by one of their ablest scientists. Immortality may be within the reach of man within 25 years. Man will be able to live for 500 years. 1,000 years, and beyond because of scientific advancements and foreseeable technologies. God in His infinite mercies is giving everybody what may be the last chance to come to Him through His Son, the Lord Jesus Christ and gain eternal life. God's technology for eternal life already exists, and He has opened the eyes of the scientists to be aware of it at a distance to confirm to us that all His promises in Christ Jesus are "yes, certainties, sureties, and Amen." My readers, my brothers, my sisters, and my friends, what is keeping you back? There is no armor against truth, and scientific discoveries of rebellious man are tramping down the falsehood of man.

God says in the Holy Bible that "He creates man and woman/" That is good enough for me. If man says that there is no creator, that he came into existence through evolution, then man has called God a liar: but the Holy Scriptures say, "Let God be true, and all men liars." Evolution is not a "proven scientific theory" as some claim because all scientific reasoning nullifies evolution. On the other hand, if we look at Intelligent Design, it is not a theory of faith as some will have us believe, but it enables us to see a "prima facie" evidence of scientific steps and facts. Does science now deny facts of the Intelligent Design of Man? Oh! In the so-called Age of Reason, man appears to have lost the thread of reason.

The Hidden Scientist Behind Evolution

Contrary to the conventional acceptance that Charles Darwin initiated the groundwork of evolution in his 1859 "On the Origin of Species," the hidden truth is that Charles Darwin is not the originator of the idea of evolution. The hidden scientist, the driving force and the originator of the Theory of Evolution is Lucifer the Devil, for the purpose of deceiving people, blinding them to the truth of God, thereby leading them to eternal damnation.

Strategies Behind Evolution

The strategy of the devil is to delude man that he was not created by God but evolved from the apes so as to make monkeys of men and laugh at their stupidity and ignorance. The strategy of the devil has not changed since the Garden of Eden. It is only refined from generation to generation to suit the prevailing circumstances; but, in the main, it is to create doubt in man as to who his creator is, and he has fallen man at his feet. Man disclaims God as his creator, and this rebellion engineered by Satan finds broad acceptance by man because he wants to do his own will. The implication of the Theory of Evolution is that since man was not created by God but evolved, man is not bound by the laws of God which demand holiness, righteousness, truth, fair play, uprightness, and justice. It is this freedom from the laws and commandments of God for people to be holy, righteous, sober, upright, just, and truthful, that is anathema to man; and therefore, the devil craftily carves the road to destruction lined with the Theory of Evolution with innocent and deceived supporters chanting the chorus of liberalism. Liberalism is the license to gluttony, sexual perversion masqueraded as a lifestyle displaying their products in the street of destruction. Gluttony befriends obesity producing diabetes, heart conditions, and other unmanageable diseases. On this road cleverly designed by Satan the Devil, sexual liberalism panders after abortions, resulting in the murder of the fetuses and babies while sexual perversion competes with AIDS in the dance of death. This is strange! Are we not in the Age of Reason? Ah! This is the irony.

According to a recent article that appeared in USA Today, "Modern biology has arrived at two major principles that are supported by so much interlocking evidence as to rank as virtual laws of nature. The first is that all biological elements and processes are ultimately obedient to the laws of physics and chemistry. Absolutely true, but who enacted the laws of physics and chemistry? A super scientist of the ages, known as the "Immortal, Invisible God Only Wise." The heavens declare His glory, but man refuses to acknowledge Him despite His presence everywhere. According to the article by the learned professor, the second principle is that all life has evolved by random mutation and natural selection. This appears questionable and off the mark. It is erroneous in two areas. The first area is that some scientists give wrong and erroneous interpretations to the observations made and the second area of error is interlocked with the first. Some scientists look only on the materials and confine their conclusions only to matter without any regard to the spirit. The spirit was in existence before matter so that without the spirit, matter cannot exist. This truth can be illustrated when we look at a dead person. Matter (that is the material body) of the individual is before us: but without the spirit, he is dead, confirming to us that without the spirit, matter cannot exist.

Therefore, matter is rooted, entrenched and enveloped in the Spirit; and science in particle physics as well as the modern knowledge of the atom consolidate this truth; unfortunately, scientists, in arriving at conclusions and inferences, miss the salient point glaring in their faces.

In the particle view of nature, scientists have found that elementary particles which are the fundamental units that compose matter do not appear to be divisible and have neither size nor structure. We can liken it to an already drawn circle that we view. When we view it, we cannot tell the beginning or the end of the circle — one of the elementary characteristics of God — without beginning, without end. Particle physics which seeks to discover the ultimate structure of matter has confirmed to us that matter is indivisible, with neither size nor structure. What other testable or repeatable evidence do scientists want to confirm the existence of God when particle physics has spoken to us loud and clear?

This is why the seekers of the truth disagree with the claims of the proponents of the Theory of Evolution that it is faulty. It appears that the advocates of the Theory of Evolution have moved away from facts of science to uphold evolution as a form of a cult society or a religious society of unbelievers steaming with fervor, relentlessly chanting "Evolution, evolution, evolution" with eyes closed or half-opened to the environmental surroundings and the history of the ages. If they looked at the environment and examined just two animals in nature to cement their observations, they surely would have second thoughts about evolution. The two animals they should look at are dogs and birds. The common experience of dog owners with the general knowledge of all establishes a dog not only as a man's best friend but the most faithful animal to its owner. Scientists themselves are just finding out some of the gifts of God to dogs. By sniffing you, a dog gathers all necessary information about you within seconds. Miracles that have happened through activities and affections of dogs have been documented and are amazing to review. Did dogs evolve with such gifts? If we are true to ourselves, our observations will lead us to accept the fact that a higher intelligence endowed dogs with such gifts. Do you not know that dogs can see what we human beings cannot see? Have you not heard that dogs could see "ghosts": or "spirits", hence they bark sometimes when they see "ghosts"?

How do animals know things that human beings do not or may not know? To give a classic example, birds know things before man is aware of them. A classic example is the case history of an incident in the Second World War. Hitler's army planned an attack on a district in one part of Europe. Forty-eight hours before the attack took place, all the birds and animals in that district disappeared. Did birds evolve to have such gifts? Absolutely not! They are gifted by God, their Creator. If we consider bird migration and how they use the stars for navigation, we can only marvel. Did they evolve that gift? No. If we look at the heavenly bodies and how the stars are suspended in space, the Theory of Evolution collapses.

We are told that scientists are not opposed to the search for Intelligent Design, only to the claim that it is supported by scientific evidence. This is great news because the Bohr Model of the atom was not only a major contribution to the understanding of the structure of the atom but also provided an explanation of the chemical properties of the elements. The idea that atoms have electron arrangements unique to each element is the foundation of our knowledge of chemical reactions and bonding. Readers, we can see that Intelligent Design is written all over the electronic arrangements of each element. Every known thing is made up of atoms. An atom is the smallest part of a substance which can exist and still retain the properties of the substance. On the other hand, a molecule is the smallest naturally-occurring particle of a substance. Molecules can consist of any number of atoms from one (e.g., neon) to many thousands (e.g., proteins) all held together by electromagnetic forces.

The positive evidence scientists miss is found in the Book of Revelation, Chapter 4:1b, "For thou (O Lord) has created all things and for thy pleasure, they are and were created." All things were and are being created. The verbs are explicit. If evolution took place, God is the supernatural force behind it. How do we know this? We believe the word of God which says, "Heaven and earth are full of God." Broadly speaking, God or part of God is in every atom that makes up anything. If God is in every atom, how can we fail to see His finger in the development (or evolution) of creatures? If God is in the cell, the unit of life, He protects the DNA and the nucleus that controls all the activities of the cell. Probably if scientists have taken cognizance of the elementary knowledge that "God fills the universe with Himself" and there is a part of God in every atom, there will be no argument about the existence of God or evolution. On the contrary, evolution could have been seen as part of the freedom God gives to all His creatures to develop in a way that gives glory to Him always.

Scientific experiments conducted by Wilhelm Pfeffer in 1883 showed that bacteria can "think," for they swam toward good food like chicken soup and away from poisons such as mop disinfectant. Pfeffer also demonstrated experimentally that bacteria can "make decisions." This scientific experiment verifies the words of the Christian song, "Immortal, Invisible, God, Only Wise..." In all life, Thou God livest, the true life of all. Therefore, the conclusion of the chapter is that we have gone through mountains and mountains of evidence pointing us to God as the Creator of man and all that exists. If evolution were true, then all the historical facts and prophecies that have been fulfilled are irreconcilable.

Let us give a quick glance at historical events. Why should God appear unto Moses and give the Commandments if evolution were true? Why did God perform everlasting miracles to free the Israelites out of the slavery in Egypt? Why did God call the Israelites "My People" if evolution were true? Why did Moses write that a prophet like unto Himself (Jesus Christ) will God raise up for the Jews? Why did God give a promise in II Chronicles 7:14, "If my people who are called by my name shall humble themselves and pray, and seek my face, and turn from their wicked ways, then will I hear from Heaven and will forgive their sin and will heal their land"? If evolution were true, why did David say in Psalm 139:14, "I am fearfully and wonderfully made"? If evolution were true, why did Isaiah say in Isaiah 44: 2, "Thus saith the Lord that made thee and formed thee from the womb, who will help thee? If evolution were true why did God say to Jeremiah in Jeremiah 1:5, "Before I formed thee in the womb, I knew thee, and before thou camest forth out of the womb, I sanctified thee, and I ordained thee a prophet unto the nations"? If evolution were true, then it means that the Holy God and all the holy prophets of God are not real. The evolutionists have called a Holy God liar and all the holy prophets liars. If evolution were true, why did God send His most precious possession, His only begotten Son, Jesus, into the world?

No, evolution is the signature of the devil, the father of lie, refining his strategies and dragging the unsuspecting human beings to rebel and deny God as the Creator and Father of us all. Let God be true and all men liars. "Heaven and earth may pass away, but the word of God abides forever and ever." Amen.

The Holy Bible: Is it an Encyclopedia of Science and a Complete Guidebook to Life?

ill it not surprise you to know that the Holy Bible is an encyclopedia to all the science disciplines and a complete guidebook to life? Forget what people and skeptics have been telling you who would like you to be in their camp, but take it from the writer, as a research post-graduate student in hunger and thirst for the absolute truth, that the writer finds the Holy Bible the divine revelation of God to mankind in the sixty-six books of the Bible, written by men, but led and inspired by the Holy Spirit. It is the most authoritative and infallible work of the ages. The writer can tell you categorically that those who argue against the authority and infallibility of the Bible do so from the platform of darkness and doubt because they have not experienced the unction of the Holy Spirit, or the baptism of the Holy Spirit, or the power of God that always makes his word a living entity. No one with an open heart and mind can read the Psalms of David, the Proverbs of Solomon, the "Magnificat" of Mary, the "Benedictus" of Zacharias, and Simeon's adoration with Prophecy without experiencing the Living Spirit of the Living God filling his heart and mind with joy, peace and happiness.

Dear reader, if these books do not uplift you, then you are certainly in the flesh, and blood with water cannot discern or understand the working of the mighty Spirit of God.

No human being who has genuinely come through the power of God can dismiss the Bible as a collection of fables written by zealots to "cow down" the people. Do you not know that the Holy Bible contains all the disciplines and professions of men in the world? Not long ago, a man was attacking the "Theory of Darwin," the theory of evolution and to the writer's amazement he said that the Bible is not a science book. That declaration shows that many people have not thoroughly studied the Bible, which is the complete guidebook to life, graciously and lovingly given to us by the Holy Spirit of God through the Eternal Word (Jesus), the "Logos" who had been with our heavenly Father from everlasting to everlasting.

In Psalm 90, Moses wrote the following words: "You, God, have been our dwelling place in all generations. Before the mountains were brought forth, or even before you had formed the earth and the world, even from everlasting to everlasting, you are God. Do you know that the Holy Bible is a scientific and mathematical book? Have you heard about the secrets of God? David in Psalm 25:14 tells us that the secret of the Lord is with those who fear him. Amos tells us in Amos 3:7 that God reveals His secret unto his servants, the Prophets. Will it surprise you to know that Adam, the first man, was a prophet (and servant of God)? Do you not know that Enoch was a prophet of God who walked with God obediently that he did not die but God took him up to the heavens? God has been revealing His secrets not only to prophets but to all those who fear Him. He revealed His secrets to Moses, Elijah and all His prophets who accurately foretold past and future events. Who can ignore all the Messianic Psalms of David about the Lord Jesus? Who can ignore the accuracy of the prophesies of Isaiah, Ezekiel, Daniel, Joel, and a host of others?

The writer is not in a position to go deeply into the wisdom contained in the Bible in just one chapter of this book but will deal with the salient points. The Bible is a Book of books. Sixty-six books make up the one Book, which is divided into the Old Testament with thirty-nine books and the New Testament with twenty-seven books.

The central theme of the Bible is Jesus Christ. The Old Testament is the preparation for Christ. As to the New Testament, Jesus is manifested to the world in the Gospels. In the Acts of the Apostles (Holy Spirit), Jesus is preached, and his Gospel is propagated in the world. In the Epistles, there is an explanation of his gospel and in the Revelation, all the purposes of God in and through Christ are consummated. Also, these groups of books in turn fall into groups, and in the past, researchers classified the Old Testament into four well-defined groups:

Group I —The Law
Group II — History
Group III — Poetry and Wisdom
Group IV — Prophecy

With the expansion of knowledge as foretold by Daniel, it has pleased God to reveal the hidden knowledge in the Bible and we now know that the Holy Bible is after all, an encyclopedia of science and a complete guide book to life. The various disciplines of science span the entire book and if Christians as well as the scientists studied the scriptures very well, there could not have been various confrontations between science and the Holy Scriptures. To put it bluntly, the science of man is way, way, way behind the science of God. One of the areas of confrontation is the age of the origin of man. Christians believe that man is here on this earth planet for only six thousand years, but the scientists disagree because they find fossils of organisms that put the age of the origin of man beyond six thousand years. The question is — Did everyone prayerfully study what is written down? Genesis, the first book of the Bible is the book of beginnings and therein is hidden the various answers to various confrontational questions. What fascinates the writer is the authoritative way in which the Book is written. Genesis 1:1: "In the beginning, God created the heaven and the earth. It is interesting to note that the Bible begins with God, not with philosophic arguments for His existence. It is expressly declared that man was created, not evolved and this declaration is confirmed by Christ. Man was made in the "image and likeness" of God. This image is found mainly in the fact that man is a personal, rational and moral being. While God is infinite, and man is finite, nevertheless, man possesses the elements of personality similar to those of the divine person: thinking and feeling. Man also has a moral nature of great significance in that it determines the boundary of nearness to God or straying away. Man is also a trinity made up of body, soul, and spirit.

Scientists have made the age of man's existence a very big issue, but they overlook the whole picture of the creation. Only three creative acts of God are recorded in Genesis 1: (1) The heavens and the earth; (2) Animal life (Genesis 1:20-21); and (3) Human life. The first creative act refers to the <u>dateless</u> past. The earth was created perfect; however, after an indefinite period of time, most possibly in connection with Satan's sin of rebelling against the Most High God, judgment of God fell upon the earth and "it became without form and void." We are not told whether man or woman or living organisms existed at that time. What we can <u>infer</u> from the information that followed suggested existence of life, and the writer hopes to expand on this later.

When the earth became void and without form, there was another <u>indefinite period of time</u> that elapsed after which "the Spirit of God moved on the surface of the waters" in a recreation of the earth (Genesis 1:2). There is very strong and compelling evidence for this viewpoint:

1) Only the earth and "NOT the universe is said to have been "without form and void."

2) The face of the earth bears "the marks of catastrophe."

3) The word rendered "was" may also be translated "became" without form and void.

This being the case, then it is not surprising that fossils found by scientists indicate existence of "Homo sapiens" — man, thousands of years older than the modern-created man. How do we know this? Genesis 1:2 tells us that the "Spirit of God" moved upon the face of waters. We know, therefore, that the seas and oceans were in existence and most probably some forms_of life in the sea not mentioned. The point is that what is revealed to us belongs to us and our children as Moses wrote, but there are certain things or secrets which were not revealed at that point in time, and they belong to God. However, since the devil does not stop deceiving man, it has pleased God that this new information be known. In the year 2005, scientists have determined that human fossils found in Ethiopia in 1967 are 195,000 years old, 65,000 years older than first thought. The revised date, they said, makes the skulls and bones the earliest known remains of modern Homo sapiens.

The research reinforces the theories of an African origin for modern humans who spread out of Africa to Asia and Europe. The findings were announced by a research team led by Dr. Ian McDougall of the Australian National University in Canberra, Australia.

Bio-molecular research on the genetic diversity among human population pointed to a common maternal ancestor in Africa, which inevitably became known as the African Eve. This evidence puts the origin of modern humans at 150,000 to 200,000 years.

Now, could this figure of 200,000 years old come from the "earlier creation" that disappeared because the earth became without form and void?

The evidence of re-creation points to that direction. This means that the Holy Bible is right about the age of the modern man. It is amazing that people do not see science from the written Word of God. Creation itself is super science exceeding the science of man. Let us try and translate certain verses of Genesis into scientific language.

The "Spirit of God" moved upon the surface of waters. We can write this as Spirit of God equals "Force" or "the Force" which is Mass times Acceleration (F= Ma) "moved" (energy of motion known as kinetic energy). We know that water is a compound containing two molecules of hydrogen to one molecule of oxygen. Therefore, we can say that when the "Force moved, energy was used, and when the command, "Let there be Light" was given, there followed all sorts of activities that resulted in the creation of Light.

The rest of the work of creation is well written in the Book of Genesis. We can never find out God's ways. St. Paul put it very well in Romans 11:33. "Oh, the depth of the riches both of the wisdom and knowledge of God! How unsearchable are His judgments, and His ways past finding out."

Why is the Bible written? The answer is so simple that you wonder if it is really true. The Holy Bible is written to guide man through life here on earth and to teach him the importance of relationships between him and God and between men and men. The Holy Bible or the Word of God is a precious gift of God to help us know Him, know ourselves, and have life more abundantly by enjoying all the good things of life God created for us. Have you ever thought of the assorted and various kinds of fruits and vegetables God created for us to enjoy? Medical knowledge and science now tell us the health benefits of the "goodies."

Do you know why light was created first? There are many reasons, but one of the chief reasons is to initiate the process of photosynthesis — the process whereby the power or force of God makes green plants combine water and carbon dioxide to make food for us.

Will it surprise you to know that the "force" or "power of God" directs the sperm into the ovum and when fertilization occurs, the "force" or "power of God" implants the zygote in the womb of the mother, and everything goes according to the DNA blueprint for the individual? Do you not know that the Christian song says, "in all life" God is the true life? Do you not know that God fills Heaven and earth with Himself?

Let us quickly go back to the nucleus of the chapter — that is that the Holy Bible is the complete guidebook to life. The Ten Commandments called LAW are meant for the protection and benefits of man and, if we go through them, we shall see the love of God hidden behind every Law. The first commandment — "Thou shalt have no other gods before me" — is meant to protect His people from the various deceptions that were prevalent at that time. Almost every one of the pagan world had a household god that controlled his actions and life. These household gods were worthless and powerless but were marketed by the people as an essential "help." By focusing on the only true God, the people would be delivered from the deceptions of the god sculptors. God has already demonstrated His power in the ten plagues against Egypt. They were indeed the true God's judgment against the false gods of Egypt. When God turned the River Nile water into blood, He was acting against Hapi, the Egyptian god, who was honored as the giver of life. When the river turned to blood, it was no longer able to give life. When Egypt was filled with frogs, God shows that the frog-headed goddess Hekt, responsible for creation and fertility, could not even control the fertility of frogs. The massive death of Egypt's cattle was an attack on Hathor. Hathor was the cow-headed goddess of love, one of the oldest Egyptian gods, and the one that was worshipped by Pharaoh. The hail was God's judgment against the sky goddess Nut who was also mother of the sun-god. It was her job to protect the land from destruction that came from the heavens. Finally, the death of Pharaoh's first-born and then Pharaoh, both considered living gods, left no doubt about the all-powerful nature of Israel's true God.

The commandment to keep the Sabbath day holy and to not work but rest is health related. People must work for six days but rest on the seventh day. Our medical knowledge of the importance of rest in the maintenance of good health shows that the God of Love who gave the commandment had the health and well-being of His people at heart when that commandment was given. Therefore, that commandment is not a punitive commandment but a beneficial commandment.

The commandment to "Honor your father and your mother that your days may be long upon the land which the Lord your God gives you" is another beneficial commandment which teaches respect and obedience, as well as the promise of longevity of life by God. Just imagine what it would be like if all of us were to love our fathers and mothers and respect them as ordained by God. What a wonderful world it would be. Hidden under the promise of longevity of life when you honor your parents is one of the undisclosed eternal laws Of God that is immutable. God rules the universe by immutable laws. Underneath this law is the principle of cause and effect, and this introduces the validity of inescapable consequences of our choices or decisions. If we make the right choices, the consequences are beneficial; but if we make the wrong choices, the consequences can be disastrous, and this principle holds good for all purposes of life.

The Lord Jesus Christ summarized for us the law and the prophets — love God and love your neighbor as yourself. Therefore, the Holy Bible is a complete guidebook to life, and it is about relationships — the relationship between man and God and the relationship between man and man. In the Holy Bible, God gives us knowledge of Himself because He wants us to have a good relationship with Him. He reveals His attributes and characteristics to us so that our relationship can be smooth.

1) He is a Holy God, and He wants us to be holy, too, as His children.

2) He is a God of Love, and He loves us so much that He gave His most prized possession, his son Jesus for us, so that we can have eternal life to enjoy with Him. Most comforting to know is that nothing can separate us from the love of God except sin.

3) God cannot tolerate sin, and this is the great barrier between man and God. Do you have any problems? God says bring them to me. Is anything too hard for me (Isaiah 59: I -2)? Behold the Lord's hand is not shortened....

4) God does not change. He is constant and consistent.

5) God is righteous and faithful all the time.

6) God is merciful and does not deal with us according to our foolishness.

7) God is the God of truth, and he hates lies and liars.

8) God is the God of Peace, and He hates wickedness, violence, wars and bloodshed.

In order to have a smooth relationship with God, we must know Him; and to know Him, He has given us the Holy Bible as a complete guide for us in life. It is our duty to study and know the Word of God very well for various reasons. King David said to God, "Thy word have I hid in my heart that I might not sin against you." Every child of God, therefore, must strive to hide the Word of God in his heart that he might not sin against God. The Lord Jesus Christ gave us the light when He said that "Man shall not live by bread alone but by every word of God." When we read the Word of God daily, we are Guided aright; and because the Word of God is spirit-filled, we are healthy, and He fills our heads with joy and happiness. The Word of God is marrow to our lives. Prophet Micah helps us to know what the Lord requires of man. In Micah 6:6-8, he gives us an insight to our inquiry.

Verse 6: "With what shall I come before the Lord, and bow myself before the High God? Shall I come before Him with burnt offerings, with calves of a year old?"

Verse 7: "Will the Lord be pleased with thousands of rains, or with ten thousands of rivers of oil? Shall I give my first born for my transgression, the fruit of my body for the sin of my soul?"

Verse 8: He (God) has shown you, O man, what is good; and what, doth the Lord require of thee, but to do JUSTLY, and to LOVE MERCY, and to WALK HUMBLY with thy God?

The children's song, "Trust and Obey" puts the picture in the right perspective for all of us. "When we walk with the Lord in the light of His word, what a glory he sheds on our way, while His goodwill we do, He abides with us still and with all those who will trust and obey." This is one of the reasons the devil tries everything possible to keep us away from reading the Bible or obeying God, and we shall read about that in the chapter on the seen and the unseen world.

In the Book of Revelations by St. John the Divine, we read that "Satan is the deceiver of the whole world." Nevertheless, we should be thankful to God because TRUTH cannot contradict the Bible since God who knows all things kept the writers of the Bible from error. St. Paul in II Timothy 3:16 tells us that "All scripture is given by inspiration of God, and is profitable for doctrine, for reproof, for correction, for instruction in righteousness."

Verse 17: "That the man of God may be perfect, thoroughly furnished with all good works."

This is the reason why the Holy Bible is given to us that we may know God, walk in his ways, and become perfect. This is why the Lord Jesus Christ in the Sermon on the Mount (Matt. 5:48) exhorted us, "Be ye, therefore perfect, even as your father, who is in Heaven is perfect."

Every word of Holy Scripture is inspired or "God breathed" (GK. theopneustos). Oh! Would to God that all mankind should accept this truth without impairing the intelligence, individuality, literary style or personal feelings of the human authors, God supernaturally directed the writing of scripture so that the writers recorded in perfect accuracy His comprehensive and infallible revelation to man. "The inspiration of the scripture is attested by Old Testament writers and by hundreds of instances where the expression "thus saith the Lord" or its equivalent is used.

Jesus Christ, SUPER STAR, affirms the inspiration of the Old Testament. By Means of Divine Inspiration, the writers of scripture spoke with authority concerning the unknown past, wrote by divine guidance the historical portions, revealed the Law, penned the devotional literature of the Bible recorded the contemporary prophetic message, and prophesied the future. Inspiration extends to all scripture, although a small portion was given by direct dictation of God (Ex 20:1, Lev 1: 1, Dent 5:4).

The inspiration of the New Testament was authenticated by Christ. Paul quotes Deuteronomy and Luke as scripture. St. Peter declares all Paul's epistles to be scripture.

It is because the scriptures are inspired that they are authoritative and without error in their original words and, therefore, constitute the infallible revelation of God to man.

The Holy Bible is an incomparable book and the most credible to life. Let us take a few examples from both the Old and the New Testament to confirm the truth that the Holy Bible is a complete guidebook to life.

The Psalms, a title derived from the Greek "Psalmos" is a guidebook to deal with every situation or facet of life. Right from the beginning in Psalm 1, David contrasts two men, two ways, and two destinies. Psalm 1, verse 1 says, "Blessed is the man who walks not in the counsel of the ungodly, nor stands in the way of sinners, nor sits in the seat of the scornful." This is a guide that can be summarized thus: Happy is the man who does not follow anyone to do what is wrong or keep bad company. Verse 2 says, "But his delight is in the Law of the Lord and His Law does he meditate day and night." This is the foundation of education in that it points to the road to peace, happiness, and contentment because man should not live by bread alone, but by every word of God. If man eats three or four times in a day, why can he not read or meditate on the word of God three or four times a day? As the material food gives man energy to perform his daily tasks, so does the word of God give man spiritual power and energy to withstand all obstacles of life. We have read about the "principle of cause and effect" and that every choice or decision we make in life has consequences that are either beneficial or non-beneficial.

In the third verse of Psalm 1, we see the consequences of daily reading and meditating on the word of God. "And he shall be like a tree, planted by the river of water, that bringeth forth its fruit in its season; its leaf also shall not wither, and whatsoever he doeth shall Prosper" is an education to know God and prosper. If man reads and meditates daily the word of God, not only will he know and love God and His ways, precepts, laws, and ordinances, but he will also love his neighbor as himself and there will be a great relationship between man and God and man to man. That will decimate or even eliminate most of the major problems facing the world today.

In verse 4 of Psalm 1, we read the consequences of the ungodly in contrast to the godly.

Verse 4: "The ungodly are not like the godly, but are like the chaff, which the wind drives away.

Verses 5 and 6 give the conclusion. "Therefore, the ungodly shall not stand in the judgment, nor sinners in the congregation of the righteous because the Lord knows the way of the righteous. But the way of the ungodly shall perish."

We see a brilliant illustration of an obedient believer and a disobedient rebel contrasted with the consequences of their actions. The same is true of all lives. There is a useful Psalm for every situation of life, a guide and prayer for all purposes of life.

The Psalms also include a vast body of Messianic prophecy relative to Christ's suffering (22:69), Christ as King (2:21, 45:72), His second advent (50,97-98), and, fundamentally, the brief 110th Psalm, depicting Christ as the son of God and priest after the Order of Melchizedek, a Psalm more frequently quoted in the New Testament than any other one chapter of the Old Testament. Highly significant is the fact that there are one hundred and eight-six quotations from the Psalms (Psalter) in the New Testament writings.

If we move from the book of Psalms to the book of the Proverbs written by Solomon (son of King David) and others, we see a collection of sayings in which, by comparison or contrast, some important truth of life is set forth. Although proverbs were common to all nations of the ancient world, the Bible's particular collection was made for the most part by Solomon who is credited with over three thousand spoken proverbs. Among the virtues commended in the Book of Proverbs are the pursuit of wisdom, filial piety, liberality, domestic faithfulness, and honesty in business relationships. Imagine what a different world we would have if people read, meditated, and followed the guidelines contained in the Proverbs.

There are vices condemned in the Book of Proverbs; among them are intemperance in eating and drinking, licentiousness, falsehood, sloth, contentiousness, and the keeping of bad company.

It would not be out of place to stop here and give a second look at the vices condemned in Proverbs, ten centuries before Christ. Overeating and drinking are big social problems in many nations of the world today. In the USA, overeating has led to obesity with accompanying heart and other deadly diseases across the board. More frightening is the release of a study concerning the youths in America. The increase in the number of U.S. children who have become overweight or obese in the past decade has been accompanied by a disturbing increase in their blood pressure levels, researchers reported. An analysis of data from nationally representative surveys of more than 5,000 children found for the first time that average pediatric blood pressure rates nationwide are increasing. With children increasingly being diagnosed with an adult form of diabetes, the new finding is another indication that the nation's obesity epidemic may be predisposing a generation to diseases that once afflicted primarily older adults. Once again, we see here the wisdom of Solomon, the writer of the Book of Proverbs, for his spiritual insight and his scientific knowledge not acknowledged until recently.

We were also given the guidelines in Proverbs to avoid excessive drinking because of its serious consequences. Listen to the headline news: "University Leaders Battle Student Drinking in the U.S." There are over 1,400 alcohol-related deaths each year among college students, mainly in automobile accidents. All over the world, excessive alcohol use has caused untold miseries. Homes are broken, marriages are shattered, abuse reigns supreme in those homes still trying to be whole, and the list goes on. Yes, the Holy Bible is a complete guidebook to a happy life.

Does the writer need to mention another vice condemned in the book of Proverbs? What of licentiousness and sloth? Well, the spread of AIDS all over the world as a consequence of licentiousness and sloth need not be over-emphasized.

What of the warnings against falsehood and contentiousness? Falsehood is responsible for countless problems and crime with miseries all over the world. Contentiousness breeds unhappiness and affects the health of everyone concerned. We had these guidelines centuries ago, and we have not listened. What is wrong with us? Who says the

Holy Bible is a collection of fables? The Holy Bible is the complete guidebook to a happy life!

Finally, the Book of Proverbs warns us about the consequences of keeping bad company. It is well known to all parents and children alike all over the world, "One bad apple will affect all the good apples," a scientific fact known by all the nations of the ancient world even the scientific confirmation of the processes involved. These days, we address "bad company" as "peer pressure" among the young, but bad company is not restricted to the young ones alone. It permeates the fabric of the society; hence, we have sophisticated crimes planned by a group of experts in their fields as a result of "bad company."

So, we see that obedience to the guidelines of the Book of Proverbs in the Bible could have ushered in the so-called "Utopia" for man.

We leave the Book of Proverbs with Proverbs 13:1 which says, "A wise son hears his father's instructions, but a scoffer does not listen to rebuke." If we are wise sons and children of God, we should hear our heavenly Father's instructions, follow His guidelines which He has given to us in the Holy Bible as a complete guide to having a peaceful, happy, and abundant life. He emphatically tells us that we should not live by bread alone, but by every word He has given as guidelines to our happiness. Therefore, it is imperative for us to read and meditate on the Word of God every day and hide the Word of God in our hearts so that we might not sin against Him since it is only sin that can separate us from God our Heavenly Father.

However, have we not acted as "scoffers" and scorned rebuke? In order to justify ourselves, some have gone to the lowest and foulest means of declaring the Holy Bible as a collection of fables. In the face of facts, of the consequences of suffering and diseases all over the world due to the disregard of the wise counsel of God given to us in the Book of Psalms and Proverbs, we should not be slaves of truth in admitting that the Holy Bible holds the "ABSOLUTE TRUTH" of a holy and righteous God. We want "to do our own thing" because it seems right or fashionable, but we forget that we only live at most one hundred years in this world. Yet the wisdom of the ages, the eternal God, who has always been and who "He is, who He is" is wiser than we: and in spite of all our so-called wisdom and knowledge, we fail woefully to know the only True God, the Blessed Father of our Lord and Savior Jesus Christ.

David says in Psalm 19:1, "The Heavens declare the glory of God, and the firmament shows his handiwork." Readers and friends, we see all these wonders of creation and we are still blind to the only True God. Isaiah the Prophet was right when he wrote, "All we like sheep have gone astray. We have turned everyone to his own way: and that is why God has laid in Christ the iniquity of us all." Dear friend and reader, knowing Jesus as Lord is a personal relationship; and if you have not known Him or His power, this is an opportunity for you to do so NOW as you read this book. Find out the truth for yourself. You owe it to yourself to "be true unto your own self." No one is pressuring you or proselytizing a religion to you. Please find out the truth yourself now. Please do this experiment for the writer and observe the results of the experiment yourself. Before you are given the procedures or the step-by-step process, the writer wants to introduce you to the experiment.

The God of Absolute Truth and His son Jesus Christ are with you right now as you read the introduction to the performance of this experiment. You need not say it to any human being because the Spirit of God that gives you existence of life is present with you and, though you may not see Him, all your ways and thoughts are naked before Him. King David in Psalm 139 said the following words: "O Lord, Thou has searched me and known me. Thou knowest my downsitting and mine uprising; Thou understandest my thought afar off. Thou compasseth my path and my lying down, and art acquainted with all my ways, for there is not a word in my tongue, but lo, O Lord Thou knowest it altogether." Over a thousand years after David spoke these words, a woman who had suffered from an incurable blood disease for twelve years and had spent her fortunes and wealth on various physicians with no healing, came as a last resort to the Lord Jesus Christ. PLEASE LISTEN ATTENTIVELY HERE "She said within herself, if I may but touch His garment, I shall be well." She did touch the Lord Jesus, and she was instantaneously healed. The key word is that she said, "within herself." This shows three areas of importance:

1) Her faith in God and Jesus Christ

2) The abiding presence of God within the heart of the woman so that the Spirit of God read the thoughts of the woman before she touched Jesus Christ

3) An everlasting lesson for you and me of the presence of God who is faithful all the time and always rewards all who stand in faith.

With all this knowledge as a precursor to the performance of the experiment, you are now in a position to proceed. Say within your heart, "Lord Jesus Christ, wash me completely by your precious blood; root out all evil from within me, set your throne Lord Jesus in me from now unto eternity. Thank you for hearing my prayers. Lead me in your truth from now on and guide me for life. Amen." Repeat the prayer five times and write down your observations in the few lines below.

If you have said that prayer by faith in sincerity and in truth, you will experience a personal relationship with God, and Christ and your experience will be a testimony to the power and existence of God. The experience of everyone will be different, but please treasure the experience and relive it always just as St. Paul always recollected his personal experience with Christ on the Road to Damascus. This is just the beginning of your joy in Christ regardless of external circumstances. After your experience, you need to read your Bible daily, starting with the Gospels, the Epistles. the Psalms, and the Proverbs to strengthen you. Also get yourself into a Bible-teaching church.

Now that we have read and experienced the power of God, let us continue with the guidelines to peace and happiness of life as given to us in the Holy Bible. Who else can teach us but the Lord of Lords and Master of all Masters, the incomparable Jesus Christ? To enjoy life fully and abundantly acceding to the plan and purpose of God, Jesus says, "Seek ye first the Kingdom of God and His righteousness, and all these [material] things [wealth, fortunes, etc.] will be added unto you."

Look carefully at the greatest sermon ever preached, over the longest hours ever preached, and the most beneficial to mankind -- the "Sermon on the Mountain" by the Lord Jesus Christ. It gives mankind the best, most comprehensive, and most complete guidelines to every problem and situation of life.

In this sermon, Jesus reaffirms the Mosaic Law of the Old Testament theocratic kingdom as the governing code in His coming Kingdom on earth and declares that the attitude of men toward this Law will determine their place in the Kingdom. Jesus also declares that he has come to fulfill the Law which He now proceeds to do in the Sermon on the Mount:

1) by showing that the Divine Law deals with <u>thoughts</u> and <u>motives</u> as well as overt acts

2) by abrogating certain concessions made formerly because of the hardness of men's hearts.

In the Sermon on the Mount, Christ sets forth the perfect standard of righteousness demanded by the Law, thus demonstrating that all men are sinners, habitually falling short of the divine standard and that, therefore, salvation by works of Law is an impossibility.

When we leave the Sermon on the Mount and move to the Epistles or letters of the Apostles, we find everyday guidelines. In his Epistle to the Thessalonians, Paul advocates peace among believers and encourages them to support the weak and be patient toward all men. He advises them not to render evil for evil unto any man, but ever follow what is good, to pray without ceasing, to rejoice always giving thanks in everything for this is the will of God in Christ Jesus. They should prove all things, hold fast that which is good and abstain from all appearance of evil. Whoa! Certainly, this is living at the best, and no one can argue against these truths.

Finally, in the Epistle to the Hebrews, we are given guidelines for the life of faith. "The just shall live by faith" is a theme that rings from the Old Testament to the New Testament advertising the superiority of the way of faith, and faith defined as "the substance of things hoped for, the evidence of things not seen." From the beginning of time, man, through faith, has accomplished the impossible.

Beginning with Abel who by faith offered unto God a more excellent sacrifice than Cain, by which he obtained witness that he was righteous. By faith, Enoch was translated that he should not see death because God had translated him, for before his translation, he had this testimony that he pleased God. The Old Testament heroes of faith include Noah, Abraham and Sarah, Isaac, Jacob, Joseph, Moses' parents, Moses, Joshua and Israel, Rahab, Gideon, Barak, Samson, Jephthah, David, Samuel, and the Old Testament prophets. In the New Testament, we have, in the Faith Hall of Fame, St. Peter, St. Paul, James, Jude, other Apostles, Timothy, and, of course, the King of Faith Himself, the Lord Jesus Christ.

The essence of faith consists in believing and receiving what God has revealed and may be defined as that trust in the God of the scriptures and in Jesus Christ whom He has sent, which receives Him as Lord and Savior and impels to loving obedience and good works. The writer of Hebrews tells us in chapter 11, verse 6, that "Without faith, it is impossible to please God; for he that comes to God must believe that He is, and that He is a rewarder of them that diligently seek Him."

Dear friend and reader, if you have used the words of prayer when you performed the last experiment asking Jesus Christ into your heart to give you a "second birth" whereby you are born again of God, you have observed that for salvation, faith is a personal trust between you and God, and faith is a working principle in life. When the Holy Spirit enlightened Martin Luther about the verse, "The just shall live by faith," he brought about the Reformation not only in Europe, but to all parts of the world because of his faith in the absolute truth of the Word of God. What is keeping you from becoming a superman of faith? Are you not the one holding yourself back? Look up to God and Jesus, now and you will see the glory of God. Hear again the immortal counsel of Prophet Hosea, "Who is wise, and he shall understand these things? Prudent, and he shall know them? For the ways of the Lord are right, and the just shall walk in them; but the transgressors shall fall in them." The choice is yours. The writer trusts and prays that you will choose the right ways of the Lord given to us in the Holy Bible.

The Holy Bible:
An Encyclopedia of Science

The Holy Bible is not only a complete guidebook for all the problems of life. It is also an encyclopedia of science. Most of the so-called discoveries and inventions of science have been written down in the Holy Bible, but because man likes to glorify himself, he readily embraces deceptions and claims credit for the truth of God which had been revealed but rejected by many and now acclaimed by man as landmark discoveries. Let us select a few landmark discoveries and compare them with what was written.

In the scientific world, Carl Von Linnaeus is credited as the Father of Taxonomy, and in 1735, the world had a landmark discovery in the "Classification of Species." The question is: Who really was the first scientist who named and classified species? The truth is an eye-opener because it helps us understand the height and depth of the knowledge of man from the beginning. If you are an "athlete of the truth," you will be surprised to know that the first scientist who named and classified species was Adam, the first man. He accomplished that feat because he had the Spirit of God, the Greatest and Everlasting Scientist mankind has not acknowledged. If we turn to Genesis 1:19-20, we read, "And out of the ground, the Lord God formed every beast of the field and every foul of the air and brought them unto Adam to see <u>what he would call them</u>; and whatsoever Adam called every living creature, that was the name thereof." Verse 20: "And <u>Adam gave names</u> to all cattle, and to the fowl of the air, and to every beast of the field."

By this knowledge, we shall not be out of place to designate Adam a scientist and prophet of God. Therefore, the first man to give us classification of species is not Linnaeus, but Adam. However, we would be correct to say that the first "secular man" to classify species was Linnaeus (1707-1778). He invented the binomial system of nomenclature by which each plant and animal also should be known, by a name designating the genus and a qualifying adjective limiting the species name. However, as the writer pointed out before, "classification of species" was done thousands of years before Carl Von Linnaeus.

Let us look at another "secular" landmark discovery of man. The gas oxygen was discovered in the 1770's. If we read Genesis 1:2, we find, "And the Spirit of God moved upon the face of the waters." Water is a compound containing atoms of hydrogen and oxygen in the ratio of two to one respectively. Therefore, oxygen has been known by the Creator and by Adam since his existence, for he was breathing in oxygen, thousands of years before secular scientists discovered it.

To go through all the landmark discoveries would require a book on its own and would deviate from the main purpose of this book. However, the writer can tell you that "secular landmark discoveries" in biology, chemistry, earth science, evolution, astronomy, genetics, medicine, and physics were written in the Bible thousands of years before man discovered them. The writer will mention two huge landmark discoveries and compare them to what is known in the Bible. "Secular scientists" discovered photosynthesis in the 1770's, and the rules of genetics in the 1850's. Would it surprise you to know that one of the reasons light was first made was to initiate the process of photosynthesis in which simple materials like water and carbon dioxide combine in the presence of light to form complex food through the agency of chlorophyll?

As the writer mentioned earlier, it would take a whole book to delve into the details of all the science disciplines in the Holy Bible. Nevertheless, the writer would mention one special branch that is of utmost importance to man, the science of nutrition and sanitation which are health-related to man. It is interesting to note that it was God Himself who taught His people hygiene and sanitation as well as guiding them in the area of nutrition. The children of Israel were told which animals they should eat and which they must avoid. Our modern-day knowledge of food and drinks has helped us understand why the children of Israel were given those guidelines. In short, by following God's guidelines, they were immune to the diseases of the day, and this is very significant because it shows again the love of God for His people as what appeared to the ignorant as harsh laws are really guidelines to healthy living. Before we move to the next chapter which is health-related, let us not forget that the Holy Bible as we have seen it, is a complete guidebook to all the intricacies and complexities of life.

In the beginning, man was a vegetarian, but after expulsion from the Garden of Eden, God approved animal protein sources as recorded in Leviticus 11 and Deuteronomy 14 to meet the needs of a race now dependent on heavy labor, speed, and physical strength to survive. The foods approved by God in Leviticus 11 and Deuteronomy 14 superceded "the Genesis Diet."

There is medicine in the Bible which Ezekiel mentioned in chapter 47:12 of his book. Biblical medicine includes herbs, essential oils, hydrotherapy, and music therapy. Dr. David Darom has identified and photographed eighty kinds of plants mentioned in the Bible that are still growing in Israel today. Dr. Russell says twenty-five percent of all drugs still come from herbs. Herbs and spices are incredible sources of antioxidants. Medicinal herbalist, James A. Duke, Ph.D., former Chief of the USDA Medicinal Plant Laboratory and author of Herbs of the Bible — 2000 Years of Plant Medicine, states that the Bible mentions 128 plants that were part of everyday life of ancient Israel and its Mediterranean neighbors.

For educational purposes and information only, and not for treatment of any disease, some of the herbs are mentioned here. Among the herbs well-known are:

1) Aloes — for burns and skin irritation, purges the stomach, aids healing of open sores. In certain cultures, it is called the plant of life because it is used for all purposes of life.

2) Black Cumin (Nigella Satina) is used in purging the body of worms and parasites.

3) Cinnamon (part of the holy oil used to anoint the priests and vessels in the tabernacle of Moses).

4) Cumin — Dr. Duke states that his research "shows that the spice contains three pain-relieving compounds and seven anti-inflammatory properties. Sometimes, people add cumin to curried rice.

5) Dandelion — Its leaves are rich in Vitamin E and contain more beta carotene than carrots. Its roots act as a diuretic and purgative, useful for treating kidney and liver disorders.

6) Fenugreek (Trigonella foerum) — Dr. Duke reports that fenugreek's bittersweet seeds contain five compounds that appear to help diabetics lower blood sugar. The Bible calls the plant "leeks."

7) Frankincense — Used in very expensive perfume.

8) Garlic (Allium satiuum) —An effective infection fighter. It is a pain killer, it stimulates the immune system, and it is helpful in treating asthma, diabetes, and high blood pressure.

Besides herbs, the Holy Bible tells us about healing oils. It mentions thirty-three species of essential oils. These essential oils were inhaled, applied topically, and taken internally. Essential oils have the highest ORAC scores. For example, one ounce of clove oil has antioxidant capacity of 450 pounds of carrots, 48 gallons of beet juices, or 120 quarts of blueberries. If you place a drop of cinnamon or peppermint oil on the sole of your foot, you may taste it on your tongue in less than 60 seconds.

Other concepts of science entrenched in the Bible are Archimedes Principle, gravity, motion, speed, anthropometry (David and Goliath), anthroposcopy (description of physical variation in humans by inspection rather than by measurement.) The classic example of anthroposcopy mentioned in the Bible is that King Saul's shoulders tower above others when the children of Israel line up and Saul was physically different. Atmospheric acoustics (science of sound in the atmosphere) and atmospheric electricity are mentioned in Exodus when God spoke to the children of Israel with thunder and lightning. Biogeochemical cycles, ecosystem, taxonomy, diffraction, diffusion and osmosis, solar and lunar eclipses, mass acceleration, weight, mathematical physics, mathematics, mathematical logic, menopause, menstruation, mental deficiency or retardation, milk, mineralogy, natural gas, and various other scientific concepts are all mentioned in the Holy Bible making it an encyclopedia of science. Do you not know that Evolution is mentioned indirectly in the Bible and the enlightened answer is found in psalm 100:3 "Know ye that the Lord, he is God, it is he who hath made us, and not we ourselves (meaning we do NOT evolve) we are his people and the sheep of his pasture."

Finally, a scientific and mathematical fact indisputable is directly or indirectly related to prophecy which includes about 10,000 prophecies, everyone fulfilled.

Certain mathematicians and scientists concede that it is virtually impossible for anyone to make eleven straight predictions, 2000 years into the future. There is only one chance in 8x1063 but the Word of God, the Holy Bible did that hundreds of times with perfect accuracy. Surely, holy men of God spoke the word of the Bible as they were moved by the Holy Spirit. Do you remember the story of two men on the Road to Emmaus after the crucifixion of Christ? Before Jesus revealed His identity to them, He said, "0, Fools, and slow of heart to believe all that the prophets have spoken" (Luke 24:25).

Therefore, what has been written so far is enough to open our eyes to the immortal truth that the Holy Bible is a complete guidebook to all the situations of life and an encyclopedia of science to the enlightened.

The children of Israel or God's people used herbs and applied oils to various parts of the body. These oils are visible materials which perform invisible tasks of healing made visible by the effects of healing experienced by the body. So we see that the life of a man is interconnected in the visible and the invisible environment, which leads us to the next chapter of this book.

Do the Invisible Forces Control
the Visible World?

One of the most fascinating experiences of life is that man functions in the visible and in the invisible world. This ability to function in the dual world is certainly a testimony to the wisdom and designer of man. Duality appears to be the "principle" of life almost in every area of existence but culminating in unity. A man and a woman are two different individuals; but when they come together as husband and wife, they become one and are united as one flesh, from duality to unity. This truth prompted the Lord Jesus Christ to quote the scriptures, "What God has joined together, let no man put asunder."

At this point, the writer would like to address his readers. Marriage is very sacred and is the foundation of good health, love, peace, and the joy of life in a society. When God married Adam and Eve in the first marriage, it was for life.

One of the wrong types of education this generation has learned is "cheap divorce." Any little disagreement or argument leads to the divorce court. The result is broken homes, unhappiness for both sides, but more importantly, sadness for the little children. Soap operas, television, movies, all encourage adultery, fornication, lies, filthiness, promiscuity; and the end result is AIDS and a sick society.

It is high time we look at the right type of education whereby marriage is a "sacred testament" rooted in the sanctity of life. God is love, and he upholds the sanctity of marriage because it is the foundation of love, peace, happiness, and blessings of life. With few exceptions (cases of rape), every individual is a product of love between a man and a woman (a husband and his wife). When the two come together as husband and wife, the product of life is a child who inherits half the genes or characteristics of the father and half the genes or characteristics of the mother so that the child originating from duality (father and mother) results in unity, the child of husband and wife. The study of genetics (science) confirms that when the sperm unites with the ovum to form a fertilized cell called a zygote which will develop into a new individual, the zygote receives an equal number of chromosomes from both the male and female organisms. This is a very interesting mathematical concept where one (husband) plus one (wife) equals one (child). The few exceptions are twins, triplets, and so forth.

Having established the significance of marriage between husband and wife resulting in an individual child, we must, as a society, look again at the "one parent" concept.

Marriage is so sacred that only in the case of adultery should it be dissolved. This has a very significant meaning spiritually. Scripture says, "Whoever commits adultery lacks understanding because he destroys his own soul." This highlights the spiritual importance of marriage. As St. Paul put it in I Corinthians 13: 1-end, "Though I speak with the tongue of men and angels..." Love does not fail. Husband and wife must practice the principle of "give and take" and should work out all problems in the spirit of love.

In the New Testament, the other condition by which divorce can be allowed is "irreconcilable differences," the harbinger of abuse, beating, constant disturbance, etc. Under those terrible conditions, divorce may be allowed because "God has called us to peace and not war." If marriage is cemented in love, there should be no room for physical abuse, mental abuse, beating and constant confrontations that so often lead to irreconcilable differences, precipitating all ugly circumstances.

God the Maker and Creator of Adam in His wisdom said that it is not good for man to be alone, so He provided Eve for Adam as a companion, a wife, a helper, and a friend. This should teach us that a man without a wife is incomplete and a woman without a husband is incomplete. The problem is that because we are sons and daughters of impatience, we look for partners who may turn out to be unsuitable for us, hence some end up in being one parent, mother or father, as the case may be. Therefore, the lesson we should learn to avoid being one parent families is to adhere to the guidelines given to us in the book of life (the Holy Bible). If we really trust in God, we shall never be disappointed.

The science of genetics explains to us how living organisms pass on their special features to the next generation. You may have been told that you have your mother's eyes, your father's height, your grandfather's red hair, and so on. These observations can lead us to appreciate and understand many things. If we know the science of genetics, then we will be able to understand life. We shall then appreciate the Ten Commandments given to the children of Israel. We will be in a position to understand the reason the Creator demands holiness from us — because He is holy and, as His true children, He demands, commands, and expects holiness from us since we "were created in His own image." If we understand the science of genetics, we shall be in a position to conclude without any hesitation the claims of the Lord Jesus Christ that "He is the only sure way back to God." Genetics also confirms the principles and tenets of the Christian religion, and the medical world has inadvertently consolidated the great benefits of Christ offered to mankind irrespective of race, color, or culture.

The statements just written need explanation and clarification. Scientists have identified the human genome. The writer wants to point out here that what they found has always been there, only new to them and us, but not to the Creator, Designer, Author, and Director of the genome. The human genome is the complete set of genes housed in twenty-three pairs of chromosomes and amounts to an autobiography of man. It took more than a decade and $300 million for scientists to map a person's chemical code, the sequence DNA. A genome, therefore, is all the DNA in an organism including the genes that carry information for making proteins. These protein determines how a person looks, metabolizes food, fights infection, and behaves. The scientists have mapped out the visible parts of the most complex machine and how it functions. However, they did not find the invisible part of the machine that controls, regulates, and directs all the operations. Most importantly, the other invisible part unseen by the mappers of the DNA is that the whole DNA is encapsulated by the unseen forces of sin and iniquity. They cannot see these because their most sophisticated tools are not strong and powerful enough to detect the "forces" of sin and iniquity that masked the whole DNA. This is why the Holy Bible says in Romans 3:23, "For all have sinned and come short of the glory of God." Adam and Eve passed on the sinful genes (mapped as chromosome No. 3 and No 7) in the genome; and physical death (chromosome No. 14) was passed on from Adam and Eve to this day. All men and women are under the condemnation of sin and death. This is why the devil, the Prince of the Power of the Air, capitalizes and works in the hearts of what St. Paul called the sons of disobedience (Ephesians 2:2). Since the genes of sin, disobedience and rebellion were passed on by Adam and Eve, we are by nature children of wrath (Ephesians 2:3) and as St. Paul puts it vividly in Romans 1:28-32, we do not like to retain God in our knowledge; we are filled with all unrighteousness, wickedness, maliciousness, full of envy, murder, strife, deceit, malignity, whisperers, backbiters, haters of God, insolent, proud, boasters, inventors of evil things, disobedient to parents, without understanding, covenant breakers, without natural affection, implacable, and unmerciful. Why is this so? Our Lord Jesus Christ tells us that "out of the heart proceed evil thoughts, murders, adulteries, fornications, thefts, false witness, and blasphemies (Matt. 15:19). This behavior of man is due to chromosomes No. 3, 6, and 7, present in every human being.

Therefore, this confirms what the Bible said thousands of years ago that the whole world is guilty before God. As Romans 3:10-18 says, "There is none righteous, no, not one; there is none that understandeth. There is none that seeketh after God. They are all gone out of the way, they are together become unprofitable; there is none that doeth good, no, not one. Their throat is an open sepulcher; with their tongues they have used deceit. The poison of asps is under their lips, whose mouth is full of cursing and bitterness. Their feet are swift to shed blood. Destruction and misery are in their ways. And the way of peace have they not known. There is no fear of God before their eyes."

Therefore, man must be born again of God in order to be set free. This is why the Lord Jesus Christ said to Nicodemus in John 3:3, "Verily, verily I say unto you, except a man be born again, he cannot see the Kingdom of God." Nicodemus, a Pharisee, and ruler in Israel was baffled and he rightfully asked how a man can be born again. Nicodemus was thinking of physical birth in a world we can see, but Jesus was speaking about spiritual birth in a world we cannot see (the unseen world). The Lord Jesus Christ clarified it to Nicodemus when he said in John 3:6, "That which is born of the flesh is flesh (the dirty garment of sin entrenched in its DNA] and that which is born of the Spirit is spirit (the clean robe of righteousness and holiness replaces the garment of sin]."

Our Lord expounded on the existence of the visible and the invisible world by citing the example of the wind. You can feel the cool breeze over your entire body, but you do not and cannot see it. It is coming from the invisible world. If you are a scientist and argue that it comes from the southwest or southeast or northwest or northeast, the argument does not alter the truth that you cannot see it. Speaking about the winds coming from the invisible world, we know that God in His infinite mercies blesses us daily. In the revelation given to St. John, he "saw four angels standing on the four corners of the earth (east, west, north, and south — Hey! Geography in the Bible) holding the four winds of the earth that the wind should not blow on the earth, nor on the sea, nor on any tree," a confirmation of the invisible world and what would happen in the future.

There are various examples in scripture confirming the existence of the invisible world. In the book of II Kings, we read that the words spoken in the bedchamber of the King of Syria were known to Elisha, the prophet of God miles away; and all his war plans were and being thwarted. Therefore, the King of Syria sent horses and chariots and great host, and they came by night and surrounded the city that Elisha lived in. When the servant of Elisha saw the great enemy and troops, he screamed "Alas, my master! What shall we do?" Elisha, "Fear not, for they who are with us are more than they Who are with them." The young servant must have been thinking all sorts of things in his head and still anxious, but his master allayed his fears by praying for him. Elisha prayed and said, "Lord, I pray thee, open his eyes that he may see." The Lord opened the eyes of the young man, and he saw (the invisible world) and, behold, the mountain was full of horses and chariots of fire round about Elisha. Through God's intervention, the young man saw the invisible world and learned an old saying "There are two worlds in one world." Elisha by his subsequent actions taught the King of Israel one of the great teachings of the Lord Jesus Christ in the Sermon on the Mount. He opened the window of the future for all of us to see and admire. He prayed unto the Lord, again and said, "Smite the Syrian troops with blindness." And the Lord smote them with blindness, and Elisha led them to the King of Israel in Samaria. When they got there, Elisha (a man of prayer) prayed to the Lord to open the eyes of the Syrian troops. The Lord God who always performs the counsel of His faithful servants, opened the eyes of the troops and they realized that not only were they in enemy territory, they were surrounded and outnumbered by the Israelites. The King of Israel in ecstatic jubilation said to Elisha, "My Father, shall I smite them? Shall I smite them?" He repeated himself so as to have his wish, but the answer of the prophet shocked him. In a preview of the teaching of our Lord Jesus Christ in the Sermon on the Mount, the prophet Elisha told the King of Israel to set bread and water before them, that they may eat and drink, and go to their master. So, a great feast and banquet was prepared for the Syrian troops (the enemy troops). When they had eaten and drunk, the king sent them away, and they went to their master. So the bands or troops of Syria came no more into the Land of Israel. There was peace between the two nations because of obedience to the principle of "love your enemies."

Let us now go straight to the teaching of the Lord on how we should treat our enemies. Matt. 5:43-45 says, "Ye have heard that it hath been said, 'Thou shall love thy neighbor and hate thine enemy;' but I say unto you, 'Love your enemies, bless them that curse you, do good to them that hate you, and pray for them who despitefully use you, and persecute you. That you may be the sons of your Father, who is in heaven, for He makes his sun to rise on the evil and on the good and sends rain on the just and the unjust.' (What a contrast between Christianity and Islam. Jesus says, "Love your enemy; the prophet Mohammed says, "Kill the infidel.")

One of the earliest revelations of the visible and invisible world is found in the story of Balaam and his ass (Numbers 22:21-31). Balaam was on his journey with the Princes of Moab when an angel of the Lord stood in the way for an adversary against him. The ass saw the angel of the Lord standing in the way, and his sword drawn in his hand, and the ass turned aside out of the way and went into the field. The ass saw the visible and the invisible world, but Balaam saw only the visible world, and he smote the ass, to turn her into the way. But the angel of the Lord stood in a path of the vineyards, a wall being on this side and a wall on that side. When the ass saw the angel of the Lord, she thrust herself unto the wall, and crushed Balaam's foot against the wall and he smote her again. And the angel of the Lord went further, and stood in a narrow place, where there was no way to turn either to the right hand or the left. And when the ass saw the angel of the Lord, she fell down under Balaam, and Balaam's anger was kindled, and he smote the ass with a staff. God alone is the only one who can help us see the invisible world. The Lord opened the mouth of the ass, and she said unto Balaam, "What have I done unto you that you have smitten me these three dines? A talking ass is enough to frighten anyone, but Balaam was blind to that miracle, and in anger replied, "because you have mocked me, and if I had a sword in my hand, I would have killed you." There was a dialogue between the now talking ass and Balaam. Then the Lord opened the eyes of Balaam to the invisible world, and he saw the angel of the Lord standing in the way, and his sword drawn in his hand, and he bowed down his head and fell flat on his face. The angel of the Lord said unto him, "Wherefore bast thou smitten thine as these three times? Behold I went out to withstand you because your way is perverse before me, and the ass saw me and turned from me these three times. Unless she had turned from me, surely now also I had slain you and saved her alive." This is a classic story of the visible and the invisible world — two worlds in one world.

Nowadays, people are beginning to be curious about the "unseen world." There is very little doubt about its existence since what we comes from what we do not see. When we visit the doctor, he puts his stethoscope on our chest and listens to the sounds of the heartbeat. The heart within the body which we do not see and cannot see from the outside sends signals and information through the stethoscope to the doctor. Also the lungs, our organs of respiration, which we do not see but which are embedded in the chest cavity, send information to the doctor when he places his stethoscope around the proper area. In like manner, the kidneys which we do not see send messages to the doctor through his instruments. Dr. James Gills, the celebrated surgeon in his book, *The Unseen Essential* unfolds the importance of the invisible things. In life, pain, fear, sufferings are invisible things that affect our bodies of the visible world, and they defy the boundaries of race, creed, color, or social status. Dr. Gills made the point that faith is the "unseen essential" that can bring about transformations and changes in life.

It is, therefore, ironical that man with all his wisdom fails to acknowledge God. David the Psalmist, tells us that "It is a foolish person who says there is no God." The Russian novelist Feodor

Dostoevsky wrote, "Not to believe in God is to be condemned to a senseless universe."

We live most of our lives in the invisible world. Our thoughts come from the invisible or unseen world. When we speak, our words are invisible. The invisible world activity is so strong that it dominates the visible world. Our invisible words can bring joy, happiness, and peace or pain, abuse, and suffering. It is interesting to note that our invisible words affect our life activities. Just as in the visible world, we speak various languages, the invisible world has various languages, but the major language of the invisible world is silence incorporated with faith.

God rules the universe by eternal laws and that also implies that there are laws in the realm of the spirit. In Romans 8, we find two laws which are both in the unseen world. The first law is the law of sin and death, and it operates in the invisible world. As the writer has already written in Chapter 2, whoever controls the heart (mind) has the upper hand. It is because out of the heart of man (that is out of the invisible world) comes evil thoughts, desire, and murder. The invisible world directs the man to carry out his evil plan in the visible world. Man operates under the law of sin and death and receives the condemnation of God. We can illustrate this better by considering an airplane in which we travel daily as part of our life activities. By the way, the plane is designed and does not evolve from a rotten iron metal. When planes are designed, they must conform to certain basic principles and laws. By the law of gravity, planes won't fly because the force of gravity will pull them down. However, when engineers give the plane the proper thrust and lift, the plan erases the force of gravity, and it flies.

We know that iron metal or steel when placed in water would sink, but big ocean liners and big carnival ships which are made of iron, steel and other heavy materials do not sink but float on the seas. Again we see that one law of science can be altered or erased by another. Gravity can be likened to the law of sin and death in that it keeps things earth bound.

However, the second law mentioned in Romans 8 is the "law of the spirit of life" in which Christ Jesus supersedes the law of sin and death. The law of the spirit of life is like the law of aerodynamics that maintains a plane in flight and keeps things heaven bound. The law of the spirit of life operates in the unseen world of the hearts and minds of men through the precious blood of the Lord Jesus Christ; and that is why everyone who professes himself or herself a Christian must be born again. The reason is not far to see. There is an inborn tendency to evil in all men as the writer already pointed out in the gene inheritance.

Besides the two laws already mentioned in Romans 8, there are four more laws which are differentiated in Romans:

1) The law of Moses which condemns and pronounces the whole world guilty before God

2) The law as a principle (Romans 3:21)

3) The law of faith which excludes self-righteousness (Romans 3:27)

4) The law of the mind, which consents to the law of Moses. but cannot do it because of the law of sin in the members.

From the six laws differentiated we see the importance of the law of the Spirit which has power to deliver the believer from the law of sin which is in his members, and his conscience from condemnation by the Mosaic Law. Moreover, the Spirit works in the yielded Christian, that is, the born-again Christian, the very righteousness which Moses' law requires. All these laws operate first in the invisible or unseen world but manifest through actions in the visible or seen world.

Let us take, for example, the law of faith as demonstrated by the healing of a certain woman with an issue of blood disease who had spent fortunes from physician to physician but came to Jesus as a last resort. She believed "within herself" with the silent language of the unseen or invisible world that "If I may touch but his clothes, I shall be well." The woman knew the law of faith and applied it. This brings to us all that it is not <u>knowledge</u> of the law of faith that matters but it is the <u>application</u> of the knowledge of faith that is victorious. The Amplified Bible defines faith this way in Hebrews 11:1, "Now faith is the assurance (the confirmation, the title-deed) of the things we hope for, being the proof of things we do not see and the conviction of their reality — faith perceiving as real fact what is not revealed to the senses." Faith — the invisible quality is so important. The woman with the issue of blood disease touched the garment of Jesus and was instantaneously healed. The story tells us that Jesus, who immediately knew that power

THE GREATEST HUMAN DECEPTION

had gone out of Him, turned about in the crowd and said, "Who touched my clothes?" Think about the phrase, "Power had gone out of Jesus." That power was unseen by anyone in the crowd; however, the woman who was healed felt the power within her though she did not see it but experienced it. The woman nervously came out, identified herself to Jesus and told Him the whole truth. Jesus commended her and said to her, "Daughter, your faith has made you well. Go in peace and be healed completely."

If we look closely at the word "power" that went out of Jesus in a scientific way, it will help us to appreciate the miracle. "Power" in mathematics is that which is represented by an exponent or index, denoted by a superior small numeral. A number or symbol raised to the power of 2, that is, multiplied by itself, is said to be squared (for example 32, x2), and when raised to the power of 3, it is said to be cubed (for example 23 , y3). in optics is a measure Power the amount by which a lens will deviate light rays. A powerful converging lens will converge parallel rays steeply, bringing them to a focus at a short distance from the lens. The unit of power is the diptre, which is equal to the reciprocal of focal length in meters. By convention, the power of a converging (or convex) lens is positive and that of a diverging (or concave) lens is negative.

"Power" in physics is the rate of doing work or consuming energy. It is measured in watts (joules per second) or other units of work per unit time. If the work done or energy consumed is W joules, and the time taken is t seconds, then the power P is given by the formula:

$$P = W/t$$

We can liken Jesus in this miracle to the power station building where electrical energy is generated from another form of energy, the Holy Spirit of the Father who performed the miracle on the woman with the issue of blood. The whole miracle illustrates the visible (seen) and the invisible (unseen) world, emphasizing, once again, two worlds in one world.

There is always strife between the seen world and the unseen world of man. St. Paul the apostle climaxed this for us when he wrote in Ephesians 6:12, "For we wrestle not against flesh and blood, but against principalities, against powers, against the rulers of the darkness of this world, against spiritual wickedness in high places." These are in the invisible or unseen world, and they affect the lives of all people. How do they affect the lives of all people? St. Paul supplies us with the answers in Romans 7:15-25. Please, this is very important and should be read and studied carefully. No one will argue with the fact that the faithful apostle of Jesus Christ speaks for us all when he said:

Verse 15: "For that which I do, I understand not; for what I would that do I not; but what I hate, that do I.

Verse 16: "If then, I do that which I would not, I consent unto the law that is good."

Verse 17: "Now, then, it is no more I that do it, but sin that dwells in me."

Verse 18: "For I know that in me (that is in my flesh) dwells no good thing; for to will is present with me, but how to perform that which is good, I find not.

Verse 19: "For the good that I would, I do not: but the evil which I would not, that I do."

Verse 20 "Now if I do that I would not, it is no more I that do it, but sin that dwelleth in me."

It will not be out of place at this time to ask what is sin? Sin is:

1) Transgression, an overstepping of the law, the divine boundary between good and evil (Psalm 51: 1, Romans 2:23)

2) Iniquity, an act inherently wrong, whether expressly forbidden or not (Romans 1:21-23)

3) Error, a departure from right (Romans 1:18, I John 3:4)

4) Missing the mark, a failure to meet the divine standard (Romans 3:23)

5) Trespass, intrusion of self-will into the sphere of divine authority (Ephesians 2:1)

6) Lawlessness or spiritual anarchy (I Timothy 1:9)

7) Unbelief or an insult to the divine veracity (John 16:9). What or where is the origin of sin? Sin

1) Originated with Satan (Isaiah 14:12-14)

2) Entered the world through Adam (Romans 5:12)

3) Was and is universal, Christ alone excepted (I Peter 2:22)

4) Incurs the penalties of spiritual and physical death (Genesis 2:17, 3:19; Ezekiel 18:4, 20; Romans 6:23)

5) Has no remedy but in the sacrificial death of Christ (Acts 4:12, Hebrews 9:26) availed of by faith

We can, therefore, summarize sin as threefold:

The important point to remember is that all these activities exist in the unseen or invisible world, but their activities are manifested in the seen or visible world. It is, therefore, not surprising that in Romans 7:21 Paul writes, "I find then a law then when I would do good, evil is present with me."

Verse 22: "For I delight in the law of God after the inward man."

Verse 23: "But I see another law in my members, warring against the law of my mind, and bringing me into captivity to the law of sin which is in my members."

Verse 24: "Oh, wretched man that I am! Who will deliver me from the body of this death?"

Verse 25: "I thank God through Jesus Christ, our Lord. So, then, with the mind, I myself serve the law of God, but with the flesh the law of sin."

We see, therefore, that mankind is under the captivity of the devil through the heart and mind, and it is of paramount importance to be set free from the invisible chains and fetters of Satan the devil. One of the great deceptions of the devil is that since he and his fallen angels and cohorts operate in the unseen world many people do not believe in the existence of Satan the devil because they do not see him. However, we have instances of his operations in the scriptures. In the last Passover of Jesus and His disciples, we see that Satan entered into the heart of Judas Iscariot (John 13:26-27) after the latter received the sop from Jesus and left in pursuance of his betrayal action. It is incredible that people see wickedness, evil, malice, hatred and cannot understand that there are unseen forces behind them that operate from the unseen or invisible world.

Since mankind places so much confidence in science, let us look at some of the forces. They are invisible or unseen to the naked eye, meaning that they operate in the unseen world, but are manifested in the seen world. Science defines "force" as "any influence that tends to change the state of rest or the uniform motion in a straight line of a body." There are "Fundamental Forces" in physics, the four fundamental interactions believed to be at work in the physical universe. There are two long-range forces: gravity, which keeps the planets in orbit around the sun and acts between all particles that have mass; and electromagnetic force, which stops solids from falling apart and acts between all particles with electric charge. There are two very short-range forces which operate only inside the atomic nucleus: the weak nuclear force, responsible for the reactions that fuel the sun and for the emission of beta particles from certain nuclei; and the strong nuclear force, which binds together the protons and neutrons in the nuclei of atoms. The relative strengths of the four forces are: strong 1; electromagnetic, 10-2; weak 10-6; gravitational, 10-40.

By 1971, US physicists Steven Weinberg and Sheldon Glashow, Pakistani physicist

Abdus Salam and others developed a theory that suggested that the weak and electromagnetic forces were aspects of a single force called the and "electroweak force" and experimental support came from observation at CERN in the 1980's. Physicists are still working on theories to unify all four forces.

The compelling evidence here is that all these forces work in the unseen world but are manifest in the seen or visible world. The knowledge of the four fundamental forces can remind us and the skeptics the revelation of John the apostle in Revelation 7:1 when he saw four angels, standing on the four corners of the earth, holding the four winds of the earth, that the wind should not blow on the earth, nor on the sea, nor any tree "on the great day of the wrath of the Lamb."

Dear friend and reader, this is an opportunity for you to come into the presence of the Lord Jesus Christ who is waiting and watching for your invitation to come in. You see, our God is special. He does not force anyone because He gives us free will to make our own choices. Having read about the invisible fundamental forces of science that operate in our visible world, why don't you try again for the greatest gift of eternal life which is free and paid for on your behalf by the precious blood of the Lamb of God who took away all our sins? Please say this simple prayer of faith within yourself now and see if you will not experience the greatest power of re-creation in you now. You will notice that the writer says this with conviction because the power of Jesus is not one of probability but of surety and certainty. What is holding you back? Please do not hold yourself back but listen to the voice saying, "Come unto me all that labor and are heavy laden, and I will give you rest; take my yoke upon you and learn of me, for I am meek and lowly in heart and you will find rest unto your souls for my yoke is easy and my burden light." Today, and now, is the time of deliverance and salvation. You are alone with Your Maker now and silently say these words:

"Jesus, please come into my heart now, wash me clean by Your precious blood, set your throne in me, and guide me forever; so that I become a new creature to the glory of God. Thank you for answering my prayer. Amen."

Congratulations, your prayers have been answered because you prayed to the One by whom all things were created, that are in heaven, and earth, visible and invisible, whether they be thrones, or dominions, or principalities, or powers — all things were created by Him, and for Him (Colossians 1:16). Welcome to the family of God and if the unseen world baffles you, remember that now that you have been justified by faith in the blood of Jesus, you should thenceforth live by faith because the scripture says, "The just shall live by faith."

There are many miracles in the visible and invisible world that you should be aware of. Perhaps, the best miracle is your re-creation into a "new individual" by the power of Jesus Christ which is the greatest miracle of God.

There are many miracles associated with the saints but, of the many miracles, none is more mystifying than that of incorruptibility where bodies do not decompose after death. There are many well-attested cases. There is a magnificent reliquary in the cathedral at Goa, India, that holds the body of St. Francis Xavier, the great Catholic missionary who died in 1552 and was immediately buried in quicklime. Yet, his body was not destroyed and even today remains astonishingly life like. St. Teresa Margaret, died in 1770; her body lies in a glass coffin in Florence, Italy. Although a little dried and discolored, her body shows no sign of putrefaction. This is all the more remarkable for she died of a gangrenous condition, her corpse appearing rigid, swollen, and purple just after her death. But two days later, she had assumed the radiant beauty and fragrance of a true incorruptible. St. Bernadette of Lourdes still looks as fresh and lifelike as when she lay dying in 1879.

"One of the astonishing aspects of incorruption is not that it happens at all, but that it frequently happens under conditions that would encourage the normal processes of disintegration, including that of death caused by disease and burial in close proximity to other bodies that decomposed normally. Some, like St. Charbel, St. Catherine of Bologna, and St. Pacifico of San Severino, had been consigned to the bare earth without any ill effect, except perhaps some minor distortion by the pressure of the earth. Others survived if one may use the word burial in such damp conditions that their clothes rotted off their intact bodies as in the case of St. Teresa of Avila and St. Catherine of Genoa. The coffin of St. Catherine of Sienna (who died in 1380) was actually left exposed to the rain for some time before being brought indoors. And when the body of the visionary St. Catherine Laboure was exhumed in Paris in 1933, 56 years after her death, her body was incorrupt despite the moisture that had attacked her triple coffin. St. Catherine of Siena believed she bore the marks of Christ's Passion invisibly, during her lifetime, and, on her death, the wounds appeared on her hands, feet, and side. When her body was examined, and parts detached as separate relics -an act called a "translation" one such mark was still visible on her perfect left foot in 1597 (217 years after her death). Dear reader, are you certain now about the visible and the invisible world - two worlds in one world?

One of the most modern cases is that of St. Charbel Makhlouf, who died at the Hermitage of St. Peter and St. Paul at the St. Maroun Monastery in Annaya, Lebanon, in 1898. In accordance with the custom of his order, like many of the incorrupt, he was buried without a coffin. For many weeks, strange lights were seen around his grave, as in the case of St. John of the Cross, who died in 1591, and who was still flexible and moist (but slightly discolored) at the last public exposition at Segovia, Spain in 1955.

The examples of the incorruptible cited above attest to the veracity of the "visible and the invisible world." In the 21st century, Our daily lives operate both in the visible and invisible world. Telephones and cell phones we use should help us become conscious of the unseen world. The auto teller machine (ATM) and all the technological gadgets we use confirm the concept of the seen and the unseen world or the visible and the invisible world.

Therefore, we should take cognizance of the declaration of Jesus Christ who came to reveal His Father to us in the statement, God is a Spirit and they that worship Him must worship Him in Spirit and Truth." Dear reader, are you worshipping God in spirit and truth? Human efforts cannot reach the lofty height; hence, everyone needs to be born again, and when Jesus Christ is in you, dwells in you, reigns in your heart, then you will reach the unreachable sky and beyond. Rest assured that all things work together for good for all those who put their trust and faith in God. Have you been born again? It is of paramount importance that you are born again so that you can fully enjoy all the benefits and privileges of a child of God. God's promises stand steadfast and sure. He says that He will never leave us but will be our God forever and ever.

What important things have we learned in this chapter? Science admits that "energy" is what holds the electron in orbit around the nucleus. Science also confirms that electrons, protons, and neutrons are made up of energy. Science acknowledges that this energy is invisible and cannot be seen with the human eye or any accepted scientific instrument. Science confesses that it does not fully understand and only theorizes about these subatomic particles or energy. Nevertheless, we see the effects of this energy all around us, confirming that the unseen controls the seen entities. In short, science admits existence of the unseen world.

Jesus said, "Out of the heart of man proceed evil thoughts, murders, adulteries, fornications, thefts..." These are unseen things that affect everyone. It is now known that thoughts are things. Our body appears to be a very powerful electromagnetic transmitter and receiver of energy.

This means that every thought you have can have a powerful impact on the cells of your body and manipulate your action. It may not be known that the positive high vibration thoughts can rid the body of disease because of the invisible laws of God in the environment. On the other hand, negative stressful low vibration thoughts (the weapon of the evil one, the devil) can give the body disease. Faith associated with positive thoughts produces healing because of the eternal laws and principles of God governing the universe: whereas unbelief generated by low vibration thoughts becomes the victims of the devil resulting in unpleasant results.

Dear reader, do you see the reason why you must be born again so that Christ in you, the Hope of Glory, can help you in every department of your life?

Invite Jesus Christ into your heart now for everlasting life.

Is Sickness or Disease
Attributable to Sin?

The first recorded historical evidence of the relationship of sickness or disease to sin is the story of Miriam, the prophetess playing the role of big sister to Moses, her brother. We all know how big sisters can sometimes be domineering over their junior brothers because they think that by virtue of their seniority, they are privileged to scold their brothers. Thank God, it was the late mother of the author who used to rescue him from the fury of his senior sister. We read in the Holy Scriptures how Miriam, the prophetess challenged her brother Moses, the great prophet of God and Law-Giver, over the action of the brother in taking an Egyptian woman for a wife. Firstly, she challenged the authority of Moses and accused him of taking the law into his own hands. Secondly, she reminded Moses that she, too, was a prophetess and God spoke to her. The root of her objection was racial because the woman in the was an Egyptian. God intervened in a timely manner for the following reasons:

1) Miriam's accusation was very disrespectful to Moses and the Egyptian wife of Moses.

2) Miriam's action was rebellious against Moses and God though Miriam may not have grasped that consequence. She overstepped her bounds when she reminded Moses that she was also a prophetess and God spoke to her, too, and Moses was not the only servant being used by God.

3) Unknown to Miriam, her rebellion was not against Moses alone but against God, too. It was not the place of Miriam to rebuke Moses her brother because if Moses did what was wrong in taking the Egyptian woman as a wife, God Himself could have corrected and guided Moses.

4) Miriam's attitude and rebellion could certainly have encouraged more rebellion and given comfort to the opponents of Moses.

5) Miriam's main accusation and objection was rooted in racism, which is unacceptable to God since He is the Creator of all races.

We read in the story that Miriam received the instant judgment of God and was stricken with leprosy and confined to the isolation unit of the camp. This story brings out certain facts:

1) Miriam's disease of leprosy was related to her sin of rebellion against Moses and God.

2) The existence of a "hospital" or unit of isolation for "Infectious Diseases" reveals the depth of medical knowledge at that time.

We see from this story that disease is related to sin. In the Gospel, we see a confirmation in the story of the man healed by the Lord Jesus Christ. In the eye-witness account of St. Mark as recorded in the Gospel of Mark 2:3-5, when the paralytic man was lowered from the roof to the feet of Jesus, we hear the relationship of sin to sickness. In Mark 2:5, we read thus: "When Jesus saw the faith, he said unto the sick of the palsy, 'Son, thy sins are forgiven thee.'"

Sin is certainly interrelated to sickness/disease when we bear in mind that sin appears in three forms according to the Lord's teaching:

1) Sin appears in human nature — "out of the heart,"

2) Sin appears in the human mind —"evil thoughts," and

3) Sin appears in human action — adulteries, fornications, murders, and so forth.

Even though sin can be the harbinger of disease, not all diseases are sin-related and there are sometimes exceptions to the rule. For example, in the beautiful story of the healing of the man born blind, the disciples asked Jesus who did sin? Was it the blind man or his parents that he was born blind? Jesus answered, "Neither hath this man sinned, nor his parents, but that the works of God should be made manifest in him." When the Pharisees challenged the man, he testified that "a man who is called Jesus made clay, and anointed mine eyes, and said to me, 'Go to the pool of Siloam, and wash,' and I went and washed, and received my sight." The Pharisees did not believe the story. They subjected the healed man to draconic questioning, but the man truthfully answered their questions. Funny, the world has not changed; the world refuses to accept the truth that God creates man and can heal any sick person according to His pleasure and mercies and goodwill. The world is prepared to go to any length to prove that truth is a lie and falsehood is the truth.

We see this in the "hallowed" Theory of Evolution proposed by Darwin and held "sacred" as the truth by all the followers, so-called scientists who should have known better. Do you see the similarities between the Jews, the High Priests, the scribes, and the unbelieving scientists of our day? In the days of Jesus, the High Priests, the Pharisees, the Jews were supposed to be the custodians of the oracles of God and in the face of the truth and compelling witnesses named below, they rejected the truth.

1) The prophecies of all the prophets beginning from Moses to Malachi pointed to the Lord Jesus Christ as God's unique son who would come to save His people from their sins.

2) John the Baptist who bore the truth and confirmed that at the baptism of the Lord Jesus. John saw the Heavens opened and the Spirit of God descended like a dove on Jesus, and there was a voice form Heaven saying, "This is my beloved son, in whom I am well pleased."

3) The works of Jesus. The miracle works that Jesus was doing among the communities, healing the sick and suffering, testified that He is the Promised Messiah.

4) The Father Himself. God the Father Himself revealed that Jesus is His son on the Mount of Transfiguration when Peter, James, and John were witnesses to the transformation of the Lord Jesus. The voice of God from Heaven declared, "This is my beloved son. Hear Ye Him."

5) The Holy Scriptures. The Holy Scriptures testify of Jesus as the Son of God.

Despite all these witnesses, the High Priests and others were bent on protecting their own interests rather than giving praise to God and acknowledging the truth. They were not satisfied with the answers of the healed man. They told him that he was not blind from birth and was deceiving them. In their zeal to call truth a lie, they summoned the parents of the healed man and subjected them to various questions. "Is this your son, who ye say was born blind? How, then, doth he now see?" His parents answered them and said, "We know this is our son, and that he was born blind; but by what means he now seeth, we know not, or who hath opened his eyes, we know not. He is of age; ask him. He shall speak for himself." We are told in the Scriptures that the parents gave those answer because they feared the Jews, for the Jews had agreed already that if any man did confess that He was Christ, he should be put out of the synagogue. It is a beautiful story because of what followed. It was a trial in which the healed man was subjected to harassment. They called him again and put him on the stand. Listen to their hypocrisy. They said unto him, "Give God the praise; we know that this man is a sinner." The man rightly answered them. "Whether he is a sinner or not, I know not, one thing I know, that, whereas I was blind, now I see." They harassed him again by asking him what did he do to him? "How did he open your eyes?" In a glorifying testimony, he answered them that he had told them, but they were not listening and asked them whether they would like to be the disciples of Jesus.

You know what followed? They reviled the man and said that he was a disciple of Jesus, but they were Moses' disciples. They added that they knew that God spoke to Moses but as far as this fellow Jesus, "We know not from where he is." The man's answer is heart penetrating for he said unto them, "Why here is a marvelous thing, that ye know not from where he is, and yet he has opened mine eyes." The man went further by lecturing them on one of the basics, saying that everybody knows that God does not hear sinners but hears anyone who worships Him and does His will. Since the world began, it has not been heard that anyone opened the eyes of one that was born blind. Surely, if this man Jesus were not of God, He could do nothing. By this time, their countenance was as red as fire and with rage they tossed him out. They did what? They cast him out. He did not belong to their club.

One of the classic examples of sickness being related to sin is found in 2 Chronicles 7:14 where the Lord God says thus: "If my people, who are called by my name, shall humble themselves, and pray, and seek my face, and turn from their wicked ways, then will I hear from Heaven, and will forgive their sin and will heal their land." This emphasizes the fact that forgiveness of sin precedes healing and ties up the argument that sin is related to disease or sickness.

Another example of sin being related to sickness is found in the story of the healing of the impotent man at the pool of Bethesda found in John 5:5. The man had had an infirmity for thirty-eight years and Jesus healed him. He did not even know Jesus because after the healing, Jesus mingled with the crowd. Later on, Jesus found him in the temple and said unto him, "Behold you are made well. Sin no more lest a worse thing come unto you." When the man left, he then told the Jews that it was Jesus who made him well. We see in this story the relationship between sin and disease as well as forgiveness of sin and healing.

In our modern day, can we equate sickness or disease to sin and healing with forgiveness of sin? We must go back to the beginning or the history of man to fully appreciate the correct answers. We know that in the beginning, man was made whole and perfect by God. There was no disease, no sickness, no tears or sorrow. All created things supplied all the needs of Adam and Eve, but after the Fall, the ground was cursed because of Adam, and "in sorrow he would eat out of it all the days of his life." For those who have been asking the purpose of life, herein lies our answer. The purpose of life is to return to God our Maker in order to have peace and abundant life. As a side effect of the curse, the ground would bring thorns and thistles and Adam would eat the herbs of the field. This confirms to us that in the beginning, man was a vegetarian. The curse continues when it adds, "In the sweat of your face, Adam will eat bread till he dies (returns into the ground, for out of it you were taken, for dust art thou, and unto dust shall thou return).

There are fundamental truths in all these declarations. Today, everyone in general eats from the sweat of his face. Everyone has to work for a living, an indisputable fact. Also, we know that God used clay (from the ground) in building, creating, and molding man to his specifications.

Death entered into the world and is universal because the genes of life and death have been passed on from Adam to all generations of mankind without exception. This fact alone is a powerful argument against evolution in that if evolution were true, then the evolved man could have evolved the gene of indestructibility and would not die or be subject to death. Man who believes in evolution is, therefore, admitting that the death sentence really confirms creation rather than evolution.

We, therefore, see that it was the fall of man that brought in separation of a sinful, disobedient, and rebellious man from a Holy God. This has been and is the problem that hatches daughters of sickness, disease, war, enmity, hatred, murder, and wickedness in the world up till this day. Because the environment in which Adam lived was still pristine in natural beauty and scenery, he lived for nine hundred and thirty years.

Even in the fall of Adam, we see the unfailing love of God in that He made coats of skins for Adam and Eve. This is love in action because God clothed them. The coats of skins are seen as a divinely provided garment that the first sinners might be made fit for God's presence.

Seth, Adam's son, lived for nine hundred and twelve years before he died. Enosh lived for nine hundred and five years before he died. Kenan lived for nine hundred and ten years before he died. Mahalalel lived for eight hundred and ninety-five years before he died. Jared lived for nine hundred and sixty-two years before he died. Enoch lived for three hundred and sixty-five years before "he was translated by God that he should not see death." The story of Enoch reveals to us the purpose of life. Scripture says that Enoch "walked with God;" and his ways of truth, obedience, humility, absolute reliance on God and uprightness in every department of life moved the heart of God to translate Enoch so that he did not die but was translated into an incorruptible body and returned happily and joyously to God.

Methuselah, the son of Enoch, lived for nine hundred and sixty-nine years before he died. Notice the length of time that Methuselah lived. Methuselah received instructions and guidance from his father, Enoch; and as a result of honoring his parents, God blessed him, and he lived for nine hundred and sixty-nine years. Please note that God's eternal law of longevity of life for honoring parents had not yet been given to anyone at that time. That law was later given to the children of Israel. There was a gradual separation between God and man, and that gap widened before the flood. Lamech lived for seven hundred and seventy-seven years before he died. He was most probably the last of the early men who enjoyed the longevity of life.

After him, God saw that the wickedness of man was great and that every imagination of the thoughts of his heart was only evil. Then He sent the flood. Noah and his family were given a new beginning. Scripture records that the whole earth was of one language and of one speech. Then man began the construction of the Tower of Babel, but God confounded them and their language was disorganized, so from one language various languages emerged and that stopped the Tower of Babel.

As the separation of God and man widened, the years of longevity of man dwindled due to so many factors. One of these important factors is the gradual pollution of the environment of man. Even though there are natural pollutants, the natural cycle provides a balance that is stable. As a side effect of the curse, man began the polluting of the environment in earnest. Man who used to drink pure spring water from the hills and mountains began drinking water with pollutants that cause sickness and diseases. Is disease related to sin? Probably you are beginning to see the ensuing picture and you will be able to answer the question yourself with conviction. Around 1963, Rachel Carson in her book <u>Silent Spring</u> brought the ugly face of pollution and its dire consequences to the nation and the world.

As man wallows in sin, transgressions of God's eternal laws and principles that govern the universe increase by leaps and bounds with the emergence of devastating diseases and incurable sicknesses.

While man, on one hand, embraces science which rejects creation of man, he at the same time flouts most of the laws and principles of science that say evolution is not even a theory but a heresy and pollution of science. Stephen Hawking in A Brief History of Time in 1988 says, "A theory is a good theory if it satisfies two requirements. It must accurately describe a large class of observations on the basis of a model that contains only a few arbitrary elements, and it must make definite predictions about the results of future observations."

From this angle, when we look in a mirror at the Theory of Evolution, we see that it fails in making definite predictions about the results of future observations. The Theory of Evolution to begin with is a contradiction of the cell theory. Secondly, if we look at thermodynamic principles, which are laws governing the conversion of energy from one form to another, we find another fault in the Theory of Evolution. This is because of the fact that among the many consequences of these laws are relationships between the properties of matter and the effects of changes in pressure, temperatures, electric field, magnetic field, and composition.

The three laws of thermodynamics are:

1) Energy can neither be created nor destroyed, heat and mechanical work being mutually convertible.

2) It is impossible for an unaided self-acting machine to convey heat from one body to another at a higher temperature.

3) It is impossible by any procedure, no matter how idealized to reduce any system to the absolute zero (O°K/-273 degrees centigrade) in a finite number of separations.

If we look at the Theory of Evolution in the light of the Laws of Thermodynamics, it falls into pieces. Why? The second law of thermodynamics is just a general statement of the idea that there is a preferred direction for a given process. According to the Theory of Evolution, the process is random with no direction. On the contrary, all the laws and principles of science point to order, and as the old saying goes, "Order is the first law in heaven and man is the created being of God and must return to God in order to find true peace." We have looked at the parts of the body, and we find unity from many members. We find purpose in every organ and wisdom in every angle of examination.

Is sin related to sickness and disease? Let us attempt to answer the question. In one of The Ten Commandments, the children of Israel were told to rest and not do any work on the Sabbath. Modern knowledge has taught us that the body needs rest to rejuvenate so that when God commanded rest from all activities on the Sabbath, He was looking after the health affairs of His people. If we look at modern man who is a workaholic, the consequences are sickness and breakdown of his health. Do we not see that God's laws and commandments are for our own good? The man who does not take a break but works seven days a week will eventually break himself down health wise, and sickness will creep in. Has this man broken one of God's Ten Commandments to rest one day in a week?

If the answer is yes, then the sickness of this hypothetical man is a result of his disobedience to the law of God which is a sin and his sickness, therefore, is related to sin. Dr. Bruno Cortis, in his fine book Heart and Soul, says the science of psychoneuroimmunology is beginning to prove that the mind and body are not only connected but are also inseparable. It has been demonstrated that changes in life often precede disease. Laboratory studies have shown that the amount of stress experienced by experimental animals can induce rapid growth of a tumor that would have been ordinarily rejected. Dr. Cortis gives guidelines to the five keys for controlling stress: diet, rest, exercise, attitude, and self discipline. Dr. Cortis is an internationally trained cardiologist with more than thirty-six years experience in research and practice. We see clearly, therefore, that the laws and commandments of God are prescriptions for good and sound health. When God gave his people dietary laws, which are now famous all over the world, He was teaching them "preventive medicine." The science of man is one of probability, whereas the science of God is one of certainty and possibility. Because man refuses the knowledge of God, he gives us different theories every time. Not long ago, we were told that all disease was caused by germs, primarily bacteria. This theory has been proved to be wrong. The next theory was that viruses were the cause of all illness and disease. That theory fluctuated. The current theory of the day is all sickness, diseases, and illnesses are caused by genetic defects, and a drug is being worked on that can solve that genetic defect. Then you wonder whether billions of dollars of profit in drugs is not behind the motives of some of these theories. Why are we sick?

Kevin Trudeau in his beautiful book Natural Cures They Don't Want You to Know About, writes that "Being sick is not normal and your body is not supposed to get sick." That is very true from the scriptural point of view. God made man perfect, but sin and disobedience brought in sickness and diseases. Why do you get sick? Is it germs? Is it bacteria? Is it viruses? Is it genetics? You don't catch cancer; your body develops it. You don't catch diabetes. Your body develops diabetes. You don't catch back pain or arthritis. These are all medical conditions. Animals don't get cancer, diabetes, arthritis, or any of the human diseases. Animals virtually never get sick except when they are in captivity. When animals are under human care and get vaccine injections, drugs, and human processed food, animals succumb to many of the diseases that humans are riddled with.

According to Trudeau, the reasons you get sick are:

1) Your body is out of balance (which means it's not functioning normally).

2) Your immune system is weak (which means it's not functioning normally).

3) Toxins are getting into your body. A toxin is a poison. It is a substance that if taken in large doses at one time would cause severe illness or death.

What causes the body to be out of balance? There are many answers to this question. It could be excess of food and drink or putting toxins in the body, or not putting enough of the "right materials." It appears, therefore, that all illness is caused by two things: 1) toxins being put into the body; 2) not putting enough of the "right material" in the body.

This is fascinating because of claims that drugs cause medical problems. It is claimed that drugs only suppress symptoms. They do not treat the cause, so the more drugs you take, the sicker you get, simply because drugs are major poisons. Drugs are major toxins. In the book Overdose: The Case Against the Drug Companies by Dr. J. Cohen, M.D., 250,000 Americans die every year from a prescription or nonprescription drug. It is suggested in certain quarters that the individual that promotes itself as the group dedicated to the prevention and cure of disease is actually the group causing more sickness and disease to occur than ever before. Is this among one of the deceptions of man? Did man bring this upon himself by rejecting the ways and guidelines of God?

When Rachel Carson in her book Silent Spring first alerted the nation to the pollution of the environment, she became the target of the chemical industry. Why? She said the truth, and that was foreign language to the chemical industries. Carson had described how chlorinated hydrocarbons and organic phosphorus insecticides altered the cellular processes of plants, animals, and, by implication humans. Carson charged that science and technology had become the handmaidens of the chemical industry's rush for profits and control of markets.

Do you see a parallel today in the pharmaceutical industry where drugs are rushed to the market to drag in billions of dollars in profits without studying properly the side effects of such drugs? Rachel Carson was right because today we put more toxins in our bodies than ever before. Kevin Trudeau substantiated this in his book <u>Natural Cures They Don't Want You to Know About</u> when he writes that "Virtually everything you put into your mouth has pesticides, herbicides, antibiotics, growth hormone, genetically altered material, or chemical food additives. Even when you eat an apple, you are taking in all the deadly chemicals that were used in the growing and harvesting of that apple. All our fruits, vegetables, grains, nuts, and seeds are grown with highly poisonous fertilizers, pesticides, and herbicides. Many have been genetically modified, turning them into poisonous material. Even when you consume fresh fruits and vegetables, you are ingesting small amounts of poison."

It is estimated that there are 15,000 toxic chemicals that are allowed by the food industry to be added to food without being listed on the label. There are thousands and thousands of chemical additives put into the food and many of these additives are not listed on the label at all, according to a senior executive at a major food processing company. The point is that the chemicals ingested in the body do not necessarily leave the body. "It appears that chemical fertilizers, pesticides, herbicides, growth hormone, non-prescription and prescription drugs and food additives such as artificial sweeteners stay in the body and lodge in the fatty tissues. Since our brains are mostly fat, a large percentage of these chemicals accumulate there over the years. This is believed to be one of the main reasons that there is such a massive increase in depression, stress and anxiety, and learning disabilities like attention deficit disorder."

Nevertheless, we come back to the question of this chapter. Is sickness or disease related to sin? Since we are in the technological age and we place so much emphasis on science, it will be proper to look through the binocular of science. Science says everything on planet earth is made up of the same thing called atoms. All atoms vibrate at different frequencies. All atoms are made up of electrons, protons, and neutrons. You will recall that in the last chapter we read that science admits that energy is what holds the electron in orbit around the nucleus, confirms that electrons, protons, and neutrons are made up of energy. Medical science believes that thoughts alone could never cure or cause disease. This is challengeable in the arena of placebo which medical science cannot dispute. The "placebo effect" is when an individual is given a placebo, which is nothing, yet his disease is cured. This occurs because the patient believes that what he is taking will cure the disease. His thoughts basically cause the cure, and statistics show 40 to 50% of the cases cured, a highly significant figure. What happens in nearly all the cases is that the thought of healing is accompanied by faith and prayer which tap into the reservoir of the eternal law of faith to produce the desired result. Thoughts enveloped in faith and prayer can heal.

Stress has been defined as negative thoughts embracing fear, worry and anxiety. Our Lord Jesus Christ in the Sermon on the Mount tells us not to worry over anything in life — food, drinks, and clothes. He tells us that life is more than food and drinks or clothes; and in Matthew 6:26, He says, "Behold the fowls of the air, for they sow not, neither do they reap, nor gather into barns, yet your Heavenly Father feeds them. Are you not much better than the fowls of the air?" He adds, "Which of you by worrying and being anxious can add one cubit unto your stature? Therefore, be not anxious, saying what shall we eat or what shall we drink or with what shall we be clothed?" If we do not heed the guidelines of the Lord Jesus and engage in worry, anxiety, negative thoughts, then we violate God's principles and we become sick. Under this scenario, sickness is related to the sin of disobedience. Anxiety, worry, and negative thoughts can be conscious or unconscious in nature, and many of these negative thoughts are trapped in stressful or traumatic incidents from our past. Many celebrated doctors have found that the vast majority of people with cancer have an incident in their past that caused tremendous grief. There seems to be a correlation between certain emotions and certain diseases. It is claimed that the stress of living in today's environment is higher than at any time in history. It is estimated that driving a car for example, raises stress levels in the body up to 1,000 times the normal levels. Driving and talking on a cell phone can raise the stress level to 5,000 times the norm.

Worrying about money, arguing with relatives, friends, and co-workers, watching scary, gruesome movies, and so forth, all increase the stress level dramatically. It is very heartening to note that modern medicine is now confirming the guidelines given to us by the Lord Jesus Christ. Dr. Coldwell of Germany is reputed to have the highest cancer success rate in the country, treating over 35,000 mostly terminal patients. Without drugs or surgery, he employs the use of techniques to reduce stress by correcting a person's thoughts. The science of man is certainly centuries behind the science of God. St. John, St. Paul, and St. Peter, three great apostles of Jesus Christ, said the same thing about Jesus. He is the "Word of God" by whom all things were created. Modem knowledge now admits that "words have power." This means "words" can change the way we think and feel. We all hear the saying, "Attitude is everything" because "As a man thinks, so he is." John the beloved apostle, speaks the mind of Christ when he writes in 3 John 2, "Beloved, I wish above all things that you may prosper and be in sound health, even as your soul prospers." Jesus demonstrated the heart of God to us when He went about doing good, healing the sick and the sufferings, enlightening us that forgiveness of sins ushers in healing, peace, and blessings of God.

My dear readers, are you sick in any shape or form? There is good news for you. God is not happy with your sickness or disease. He is unhappy about your sorrow and problems. You are hurting because you do not know Him. He is not far from you as you read these lines. He is a willing God ready to help you. His promises stand steadfast and sure. His power has not changed but remains the same; and Jesus Christ His son is the same yesterday, today, tomorrow, and forever. With men, it may be impossible, but with our God, the Blessed Father of the Lord Jesus Christ, all things are possible.

Technically speaking, sickness or disease can be related to the sin of disobedience to the rules and guidelines of life. However, the most reassuring thing is that God wants for us peace, joy, and good health. One of the attributes of God o is perfection and in the Sermon on the Mount, Jesus exhorts us to be perfect even as our Heavenly Father in Heaven is perfect. We have seen in an earlier chapter (Chapter 2), that God made a perfect man, Adam was the highest manifestation of God, and Adam has been rightly called the son of God. We see perfection and wisdom in every part of our bodies. Why then sickness, arthritis, pain, backache, and old age? We have to go deep into history in order to excavate the truth. In the Garden of Eden, God warned Adam and Eve not to eat of the fruit of the tree which was in the midst of the Garden. They were commanded not to even touch it because they would die. The serpent or Devil told Eve, "You shall not surely die, for God knows that in the day you eat it your eyes shall be opened and ye shall be as God, knowing good and evil." First, the Devil or serpent made God a liar to Eve by saying, "You shall not surely die." The tactics and strategies of Satan the Devil have not changed. He distorts the truth and tells half-truths to make it appealing. The Devil knows that Adam and Eve would not just fall down and die instantaneously when they eat the fruit, but they would begin to die gradually until death takes them over. The Devil knows that God works by the Principles of Gradualism, and it will take time for them to die. We know, however, that God's word is true, and Adam and Eve eventually died and passed on the genes of life and death to all the races of man. The writer would like to mention here that Satan deceived Darwin by the distortion of God's Principles of Gradualism to formulate the heretical Theory of Evolution. The reason it is appealing to those who are lost is the presence of the gene of doubt and distrust of the truth and comfortableness with lies. In view of the fact that Adam passed on the gene of death, the process of death is a gradual process. We can use the adage "born to die" for we begin to die from the very day we are born. Cells begin to wear out and are replaced by new ones and the constant dying out of cells and other processes eventually lead to old age, disease, sickness, and other ailments, all due to the curse. Therefore, it is without hesitation that the writer emphatically submits that sickness, illness, and disease are related to sin, originating from the curse, but the Devil will not allow us to believe this because we think we are too smart. Too smart by half!

What, therefore, is the purpose of this chapter? It is to draw the reader's attention to the facts of life and reality. We see old men and women every day. We see sick people in the hospital. The nations of the world spend trillions of dollars on health problems with no relief in sight. However, recent statistics by scientists all over the world attest to the fact that among those with chronic diseases and those declared incurable by doctors, some have been miraculously healed when they go to church regularly and those who were not healed lived longer than those who did not go to church at all. Strange enough, they are baffled, and our smart people cannot provide an acceptable and suitable explanation. But thank God, the righteous are given the secrets of the Lord.

Over two thousand years ago, the early church members were exhorted by St. Peter "not to forsake the assembly" of the people which means going to church regularly. Is there any benefit in going to church regularly? King David under the realization of the blessings of God said in Psalm 122, "I was glad when they said unto me, 'Let us go into the House of the Lord?" He was in joyous anticipation of the blessings he would receive in the House of the Lord. Over the years, the "House of the Lord" is a "strong tower". The righteous run into it and are safe. The House of the Lord is called the House of Prayer where the prayers of the righteous are effective. When we go to church, therefore, we receive many blessings of life. We have fellowship with men, women, children, babies, and God with Christ. We sing hymns of praise that are healthy to our bodies and souls. We hear the guidelines of God from His Holy Word through the preaching of the minister. But that is not all. Read a great revelation only known by the few. We hear a lot about the ministry of angels of Christ, but people do not know how they function. Is there any benefit in going to the church every Sunday? The answer is YES. First of all, Jesus Christ is in the midst of the church, blessing believers with the breath of His spirit which is an energy force that burns or destroys illnesses and diseases. In addition to that, the angels of Christ come into the service three times. They come at the beginning of the service to bless. Friend and reader, please do not be late to church service because you will miss the opening blessings by the angels of God and Christ. If you are a habitual "late goer" to the church, please let that habit cease today because you are missing the first batch of blessings of God. Then, in the middle of the service, the angels of God and Christ come again and bless believers and, finally, at the end of the service, they come again and bless the congregation. All members of the congregation, therefore, receive every Sunday the blessings of the direct breath of God and Christ. These are unseen by people, but they are true and real. This is the reason those with sickness and illness who go to church regularly improve in health because of the unseen breath of God they constantly receive, and that is why the number of survivors increase.

When you go to the House of God, go with a thankful and grateful heart that you are privileged to be there, and concentrate on the service and the worship of God. You will be surprised that at the end of the service, a miracle will have taken place, and the only time you know it is when you perceive it. You may not even pray for healing, but He could heal you to confirm to you that He cares, and underneath are the everlasting arms of love open wide to receive you.

Are you a believer in Christ? Do you know Jesus? Would you like to know Jesus? He is the answer and reality to all the problems of life. He is not far from you. He works in silence, and silence is His policy and principle. He knows your ups and downs and under-stands your thoughts afar off. He says, "Come unto me all ye that are weary and heavy laden, and I will give you rest. Take my yoke upon you and learn of me; for I am meek and lowly in heart, and you will find rest unto your souls." What is holding you back? The woman with the issue of blood said silently within herself, "If I could but touch the hem of His garment, I shall be healed." She touched the hem of Jesus' garment and was healed.

Now it is your turn to say silently within you as you read these pages, "Lord, I believe. Help my unbelief. Come into my heart now. Wash me by your precious blood and make me a new creature. Amen."

Congratulations! Welcome into the family of God.

Before leaving this chapter, let us hear the latest news from the field of science which confirms that diseases and sickness are related to sin. When Moses told the children of Israel that "God is a jealous God visiting the iniquity of the fathers upon the children unto the third and fourth generation of them who hate me, but showing mercy unto thousands of them who love me and keep my commandments," (Deuteronomy 5:9-10), they did not believe him and scoffed at the idea. Over a thousand years after, Euripides noticed that the gods visit the sins of the fathers upon the children. Sharon Begley writing in the Science Journal says that scientists are discovering that nature can be even crueler than Euripides imagined. It can visit the sins of the grandparents on the children. She adds that such "transgenerational" effects are the latest focus of a growing field called fetal programming or the fetal origins of adult diseases. It examines how conditions in the womb shape physiology in a way that makes people more vulnerable decades later to cardiovascular disease, diabetes, immune problems, and other illnesses usually blamed on genetics or lifestyle, not on what arrived via the placenta. If a fetus is poorly nourished, for instance, it can develop a "thrifty phenotype" that makes it really good at getting the most out of every meal. After birth, that lets it thrive if food is scarce, but it's a recipe for Type 2 diabetes in a world of doughnuts and fries. Poor fetal nutrition can lead to hypertension, too. If it causes the fetus to produce too few kidney cells, the adult that the fetus will become won't be able to regulate blood pressure well.

In April 2005, scientists reported that a child whose grandmother smoked while pregnant with the child's mother, may have twice the risk of developing asthma as a child whose grandmother didn't flood her fetus with carcinogens. Remarkably, the risk from Grandma's smoking was as great as or greater than from Mom's. Kids whose mothers smoked while pregnant were 1.5 times as likely to develop childhood asthma as children of nonsmoking moms. Kids whose grandmothers smoked while pregnant with mom were 2.1 times as likely to develop asthma, scientists reported in the journal chest. The harmful effects of tobacco, it seems, can reach down two generations even when the intervening generation, mom, has no reason to suspect her child may be at risk. "Even if the mother didn't smoke, there was an effect on the grandchild" says Frank Gilliland of the University of Southern California, Los Angeles, who led the study of 908 children.

Sharon Begley asks, "What causes the grandma effect? One suspect is the DNA in the fetus's eggs (all the eggs a girl will have are made before birth). Chemicals in smoke might change the on-off pattern of genes in eggs, including genes of the immune system, affecting children, who develop from those eggs. Interesting data point at other grandma effects. In May 2005, scientists reported the first discovery that obesity and insulin resistance, as in Type2diabetes, can be visited on the grandkids of female rats that ate a protein-poor diet during pregnancy, lactating, or both." Peter Nathanielsz of the University of Texas Health Sciences, of San Antonio, "Stretch the unwanted consequences of poor nutrition across generations." In people, too few calories, too little protein, too few other nutrients can all lead to diabetes, hypertension, and other ills decades later. "That suggests that what links diet to adult diseases is something quite fundamental," says Simon Langley-Evans of the University of Nottingham, England. The key suspects: changes in DNA activity in the fetus or in the balance of hormones reaching it via placenta.

Alarmingly, the list of what can be passed along is growing conclusively, confirming the veracity of the Holy Bible.

Listen to the admission of science! "For most diseases, the basic knowledge of where they come from and the biological processes that set them in motion is a complete mystery. Among them are heart disease, cancer, high blood pressure, asthma, diabetes, and neurological disorders, which are triggered by complex sets of genes acting together." (St. Petersburg Times, October 30, 2005).

Are we seeing the prophecies of the Lord Jesus Christ about His second coming but are blind to them? International Disaster Database reveals that along with hurricanes that devastated parts of Florida and the Gulf Coast in 2005, nature has taken a huge toll around the globe. In a world of about six billion people, more than one billion people have been affected by natural disasters, including more than 85,500 who died. In Pakistan alone, the death toll from the October 8, 2005, earthquake is over 73,276. In the USA, as a result of Hurricane Katrina in August 2005, more than 1,300 people were killed, with damage over $100 billion. In Guyana, 150,000 people were affected in January 2005, by three days of torrential rain. In Central America, Hurricane Stan in October 2005, caused flooding and mudslides which killed over 2,000 people, most in Guatemala. In Hurricane Wilma in the US, in October 2005, there were more than twenty deaths and $12 billion in damage. Can we blindly interpret this as nature or is this the finger of God warning mankind to depart from evil?

Top Secret: Classified Until...

These words "Top Secret" or "Classified Until..." the time mentioned means that the document or information is designated as "secret" and available only to authorized persons. All the governments of the world have "top secret documents." Businesses all over the world have "top secrets" or "classified documents" which are essential to the survival of their businesses. We see in the business world such as banks, stock exchanges, and financial institutions that some people who have access to "top secret" information used that information to selfish ends and resulted in unpalatable consequences.

Government policies in certain countries and nations are "classified top secret" until fifty years or twenty-five years depending on the sensitivity and importance of the issue. It was only a few years ago that some of the documents of the second world war were released fifty years after the event.

From the call of Abraham in the Holy Scriptures to the death of Joseph, we note the existence of "classified information:"

1) God made an "unconditional promise" of blessings through Abraham's seed to the nation of Israel to inherit a specific territory forever.

2) to the church as in Christ

3) to the Gentile nations.

In point of fact, the promise, which is the Fourth Dispensation, extended from the call of Abram to the giving of the Law at Sinai. It seems as if God's dealings with man are under "classified information" and periodically the picture is released episode by episode in a gradual process. In Genesis 3:15, we read about the promises and the prophecies concerning Christ which were fulfilled about four thousand years later. Our lives are "classified information" because we do not know tomorrow, and God encourages us to have faith that all will be well. Therefore, He discourages His people from going to the stargazers or astrologers to dig out their life story because "the just shall live by faith." Right through the Holy Scriptures, we read examples of "classified information" and the unfolding of same centuries later.

However, there are three compelling examples to which your attention is drawn. The first is the vision of Daniel in connection with world empires as recorded in Daniel chapter 7. He saw what could be called "classified information." Prior to Daniel's vision, King Nebuchadnezzar had the monarchy vision which covers the same order of fulfillment as Daniel's beast vision, but with this difference. Nebuchadnezzar saw the imposing outward power and splendor of the "times of the Gentiles." The vision prophetically portrays the course of world empires and its destruction by Christ, who called this period "the times of the Gentiles." The significance of Daniel's dream is that he saw the true character of Gentile world government as rapacious and warlike, established and maintained by force. It is remarkable that the heraldic insignia of the Gentile nations are all beasts or birds of prey. The first world empire was Babylon, the second was the Medo-Persian Empire, the third world empire was Greece, and the fourth world empire, Rome or Roman Empire. Daniel saw the vision of the end of Gentile world dominion, and the coronation of the "Son of Man" as King of Kings and Lord of Lords. Daniel thus was shown remarkable revelations of "classified information." The accuracy about the reign, character, and antecedents of Antiochus Epiphanes, the Hellenistic King who cruelly persecuted the Jews 400 years after the time of Nebuchadnezzar, was used by Porphyry, an anti-Christian philosopher of the third century A.D. as proof that the Book of Daniel could not have been written before that time. How astonishing! If Porphyry had done his homework well, he could have known that God declares the end from the beginning, and if Porphyry were perplexed about the time period, he should have read the Book of Isaiah which accurately described the life and death of the Lord Jesus Christ almost 800 years before it happened. The modern supporters of Porphyry remind us of the blind leading the blind.

Daniel was shown the great tribulation and the resurrection and was told to seal the book to "the time of the end." However, Daniel tells us that one of the signs of the end time is the "explosion of knowledge" in all frontiers of life. Are we in the end times as we witness explosion of knowledge in every department of life? What is responsible at this time in the 21st century for explosion of knowledge? The scientists confirm that two genes are involved in leaps of human intellectual development, but they miss the conclusion drawn. Bruce Lahn and his University of Chicago researchers in 2005 found two key brain building genes and claimed that they provide the first scientific evidence that the human brain is still evolving, a process that may ultimately increase people's capacity to grow smarter and get smarter. Lahn and his researchers claim that these genes are still undergoing rapid mutations. Their findings are partly true, but their inferences and interpretations are off mark. What Bruce Lahn and his researchers found is actually a confirmation of the prophecy of Daniel on two fronts:

1) It consolidates the fact that there is an explosion of knowledge. However, God Himself is responsible for this act. He allows the brain to expand through the mutation of the genes which the researchers observed and confirmed.

2) Knight Rider Newspapers report that "Researchers say that one of the mutated genes, called microcephalin, began its swift spread among human ancestors about 37,000 years ago, a period marked by creative explosion in music, art, religious experience and tool making. The truth is that when God, the time-controller, determined that it was ripe for man to come into that knowledge arena, He initiated the process. Mankind in the 21st century has exploded in knowledge because of the prophecy of Daniel that at the time of the end, such would happen.

What Dr. Bruce Lahn and his researchers found are not evolutionary changes of the brain but confirmation of the prophetic expansion of the brain as revealed to Daniel thousands of years ago. It is now an open secret that science and technology are confirming mind over matter though they seem to be unaware of it. Technology has turned man into a semi-god. We have false teeth and hair, plastic limbs, intraocular lenses, mechanical organs, and drug dispensing implants. Robots are becoming more like human in facial expression, voice recognition, and ability to walk, talk, and make decisions. Sidney Perkowitz raises this question in Digital People: From Bionic Humans to Androids" (Joseph Henry Press), a book that describes how a new generation of robots could serve as "the next level of humanity." It is suggested that materials science, digital microprocessing, and artificial intelligence may pave the way to startling innovations by the end of the 21st century. It is estimated that about 25 million people in the United States are partly bionic, having artificial hardware in their bodies. As people live longer and medical technologies offer new kinds of replacement parts, people will become more and more hybrid — part flesh and bone, part wire and titanium.

In Japan, the government each year funds $38 million to the Humanoid Robotics Project. One goal is to develop a machine with the mental, physical, and emotional capacity of a five-year old. This should remind us of King David when he declared in Psalm 82:6, "I have said ye are gods; and all of you are the children of the Most High." Without realizing it, man is proving the scriptures to be true, but the sad part is that he is unaware of it. Look at how technology has affected the lifestyles of people. We have portable television, portable computers (laptops), cell or mobile phones with which we can do anything we want this day — talk, take photographs, listen to music, and manipulate them as we like. For years, vacationers have relied on guidebooks to plan trips, but because of the high cost of printing, publishers for the most part limit their books to the most popular tourist attractions and highly regarded tourist attractions in big cities and other well-traveled areas. Now, more and more globetrotters are using the web to supplement guides. With the availability of Mapquest, navigational information is made easy.

Technology has transformed airline travel, hotel accommodations, rental agencies, and every fabric of our lifestyles. All these changes around us are the fulfillment of the Holy Scriptures written for our benefit and should draw our attention to the God of Jesus Christ, the Lord God of the Hebrews who knows the end from the beginning and gave the revelation to Daniel. The stark reality is the fact that technology is only new to us but not to God. Technology was in existence before time, and we are just beginning to find out what the Creator of the Universe used when He set His Work of Glory in motion. The scripture rightly declares in Psalm 19, "The heavens declare the Glory of God and the firmament shows His handiwork."

The discoveries of man and all the research work in every discipline of life point to one indisputable fact. Ignorance is the incurable disease of man. It is incurable because man refuses the only effective prescription, the knowledge of God first. Jesus says, "Seek ye first the Kingdom of God and His righteousness and all these things (knowledge, wisdom, science) shall be added unto you" (Matthew 6:33). God wants us to have abundant life; and all the fruits, vegetables, plants, and animals in our environment are for us to enjoy. Be thankful for them and praise God in worship. Simple!

The second compelling example of "classified information" was given by our Lord Jesus Christ about His second coming. The disciples wanted to extract the exact time as they asked Him "when" He will return and "what" shall be the sign of his coining, and of the end of time.

He plainly told them that He did not know because it is top secret and classified information. No one knows the exact time, not even the angels in Heaven, except God our Heavenly Father. He then predicted that many false prophets shall arise and deceive many, and He warned the disciples and believers to beware. The Lord predicted that "Nation shall rise against nation, kingdom against kingdom. and there shall be famines, and pestilences, and earthquakes in various places." These, He said, are the beginnings of sorrow. "They shall deliver you up to be afflicted and shall kill you and ye shall be hated of all nations for my name's sake. And then shall many be offended and shall betray one another and shall hate one another

(Matthew 24) and because iniquity shall abound, the love of many shall grow cold. And this Gospel of the Kingdom shall be preached in all the world for a witness to all nations and then shall the end come (Matthew 24: 7-12 and 14).

We already witness nation rising against nation, kingdom against kingdom. We have seen famines and pestilences and earthquakes in various places of the earth. Scientists tell us that more land around the world is suffering in severe drought, and it might be self induced. The percentage of global land area hit by serious drought has more than doubled over the past twenty-five years, according to scientists at the National Center for Atmospheric Research. The reason, they say, can be traced to rising temperatures. Devastating droughts have occurred in Canada, Asia, Europe, Africa, and Australia. The question is asked by Kurt Loft, Tampa Tribune correspondent, whether this could be part of the normal, long-range climate cycle, or the influence of people? Much of the evidence points to the greenhouse effect, according to Ague Dai, lead author of a study released recently at the American Meteorological Society's annual meeting in San Diego. "The earth also is getting slightly warmer, and 2004 was the ninth warmest year of the past quarter century. The United States is understandably one part of the world that doesn't seem to be affected by the drought, but frequent and fiercer hurricanes like Katrina and Rita make us think twice.

All the predictions of the Lord Jesus are being witnessed by all, yet many are still under spiritual blindness. Today, all over the world, many Christians are killed and massacred according to the prediction of the Lord. Last year in the United States, of all places, many were offended, and during celebrations of the birth of Christ, nearly all the media refrained from saying, "Merry Christmas," so that they wouldn't offend unbelievers. There are many false prophets and deceivers all over the world, and the gospel of the Lord Jesus Christ is being preached all over the world in this age of radio, television, and mass communication through the internet. All the predictions of

the Lord appear to be fulfilled or nearing the completion of fulfillment, and we can boldly say that the "Lord is coming soon" and, therefore, "Let the wicked man forsake his ways; repent and pray to be born again by inviting Jesus into his heart." It is imperative that man or woman must be born again of God in Christ before they can forsake their evil ways.

Man does not know that he is under spiritual blindness and captivity of Satan until he is released by the spiritual blood of Jesus Christ, and then his eyes are opened, and he recognizes the fact that he had been in captivity. You need to read the testimony and experiences of chronic drug users and drunkards who went through lifechanging experiences when they invited the Lord Jesus Christ into their hearts by faith. They stopped using drugs and hated drinking because they had experienced the release from the captivity power of the Devil and his minions. They come into the victorious life of the Lord Jesus. It was after their release and freedom from the evil power of Satan and his fallen angels that they are able to see the Light of God in the face of Jesus Christ. St. Paul, writing to Titus in Titus 2:11-14, says, "For the grace of God that brings salvation hath appeared to all men," teaching us that, denying ungodliness and worldly lusts, we should live soberly, righteously and godly, in this present age, looking for that blessed hope and the glorious appearing of the great God and our savior Jesus Christ, who gave Himself for us, that he might redeem us from all iniquity and purify unto himself a people of His own, zealous of good works.

Dear Reader, do you have a weakness or bad habit you cannot get rid of and have tried various vitamins, drugs, and medicine without success? Do you have any secret you cannot tell your closest friend or relative? Today is the Day of Salvation for you. Do you always do what you don't want to do but somehow you do it anyway? Today is your Day of Freedom. The voice of Jesus is saying to you, "Call unto me. I will answer you. I will hear your prayers and set you free." It does not cost you any money. It is free. Would you like to be free now? Then, say within your heart silently or openly, "Lord Jesus, I am helpless, and you know all my problems. I believe you are the same yesterday, today, and tomorrow. Therefore, I renounce all evil same things or wrong things in my life. Come into my heart and help me overcome all my problems by the power of your precious blood and the Spirit of Holiness of your resurrection power. Amen."

Give thanks to God and praise His holy name. Welcome into the family of God. You have passed from spiritual death to eternal life through Jesus Christ. Now you need a good and sound Biblical education to cement your faith. You should attend a Bible-believing church where Jesus Christ is proclaimed, honored and exalted.

Now, let us look at the third compelling evidence of top secret, classified information, and we find this is the Book of Revelation by St. John, the beloved apostle of the Lord Jesus Christ. The Book of Revelation, the concluding book of the scriptures, unfolds the great events bringing history to consummation, including the revelation of Jesus Christ at His Second Advent. Revelation of St. John is a disclosure of that which was previously hidden or unknown. It reveals that Jesus Christ is:

1) The "watershed of history"

3) The Ruler of the kings of the earth and so He is King of Kings, Lord of Lords, and Master of all Masters

3) The bridegroom and Head of the Church

4) The Lion of the Tribe of Judah

5) The Lamb of God that was slain before the foundation of the world

6) The High Priest after Melchizedek

7) The King and Judge

The book provides the setting for the revelation of Jesus Christ which appears to coincide with Daniel's vision of the end tune. From every day's newspapers, from the radio, news media, television news from all over the world, we see an increase in wickedness, murder, sexual immorality, lewdness, incurable diseases, oppression, religious and racial bigotry, and the failure of governments, all pointing to the beginning of the end of "Gentile world dominion" and the significance of Daniel's vision.

The highest function of government is the protection of human life, out of which arises the responsibility of capital punishment. Government should safeguard the sanctity of human life as a gift of God which cannot rightly be disposed of except as God permits. The history of the governments of man reveals that men have failed to rule righteously. In the olden days, both Jew and Gentile governed for self, not for God, and this was apparent. This failure was seen racially in the confusion of Babel, in the failure of Israel in the period of the theocracy, which closed with captivity in Babylon. Now, in these times of the Gentiles, the governments of the nations of the world have failed in protecting lives. The 1994 Rwandan genocide induces shame at the memory of the world's indifference when a death toll of some 800,000 souls might have been averted. In the spring of 1994, Rwanda was a powder keg barrel, and any slight friction could cause explosions. Members and supporters of a French-backed HUTU government were unhappy at the terms of a U.N. supervised agreement to share power with a minority Tutsi rebel group. Although Rwanda's Hutu President supported the agreement, the shooting down of his plane was the signal for a planned effort by Hutu extremists to exterminate Tutsis altogether; and they precipitated Rwanda's holocaust. It is sad to note that the United Nations, Belgium, and France, all of which had a military presence in Rwanda, failed to act; and America was reluctant to shoulder the responsibility and take the lead. On that note, the Gentile nations of the world failed to protect the sacred lives of those massacred. We have heard about recent genocide in Sudan. The governments of the world nations failed to act in due time, and there are other specific cases in other parts of the world which are beyond the scope of this chapter. It is, therefore, evident that man has failed to rule righteously. The days of man's rule are numbered, and his rule will be superceded by the glorious reign of our Lord Jesus Christ whose right to rein is uncontestable, for He is the incomparable Christ.

So, dear reader, where do you stand? Are you in Christ? He is not far from you. Invite Him by faith into your heart and your life will never be the same again.

The Culture of Death

There has recently been a legal case about the wishes of man in certain critical decisions, and this case became worldwide news. It is the case of a husband who wanted to remove feeding tubes from his wife because some medical doctors testified that she was in a vegetable state. According to the husband, he was acting on the wishes of his wife, to kill the latter. However, the parents of the wife wanted their daughter back and not killed. There ensued epic court battles between the husband on one side advocating the removal of the lifeline of food and drink, and on the other side, the parents of the wife, begging frantically for the preservation of the life of their daughter. The outcome was a victory for the husband, resulting in the removal of the feeding tubes and the woman's starving to death. The case highlights the wishes and desires of man against the guidelines and commandments of God, the Giver of Life.

Thomas Jefferson, almost three hundred years ago, declared that "the first duty of government is the protection of life, not its destruction. The chief purpose of government is to protect life. Abandon that, and you have abandoned all. It was Jefferson who, in penning the words of the Declaration of Independence, declared that the right to life was "endowed" to us by our Creator. Government's role, according to this revered founding father, was to "secure" the "unalienable" rights conferred by the Creator. There is a reason for such primacy to the right of life, the "first" right, without which all other rights are meaningless.

The founding fathers of America knew that "the highest function of government is the protection of human life." To speak as one pleases, to worship as one chooses, and to associate with those whom one prefers, all depend upon the protection of the right to life. Ken Connor, a Florida trial lawyer and chairman of the Center for a Just Society, wrote an article in the Tampa Tribune of March 27, 2004, in which he says, "Historically, courts have been a bastion for the protection of individual liberties — the great 'equalizer' for the vulnerable and the poor. However, increasingly around the country, courts are becoming abiders and abettors of the strong in exploiting the weak." Ken Connor continues, "As our country shifts away from a sanctity-of-life ethic and moves increasingly toward an ethos that uses cost-benefit ratios and 'quality-of-life' calculus to calculate the net worth of individuals, who will protect us from exploitation and abuse when we become inconvenient or when we cost more to maintain than we produce? If not the government, who will stand in the gap?"

The answer is simple. God who delegated man and instituted a corporate relationship of man to man in human government will step in. We are seeing the fulfillment of all the prophecies written in the Holy Scriptures about the end of times. Man's government has failed woefully and is failing to rule righteously all over the world created by a Holy God, and when the sanctity of life is threaded upon and the banner of the culture of death is being unfurled, then God the Father shall surely step in. He is not the God of the dead. David the Psalmist wrote, "The living, the living shall praise God, not the dead. Jesus Christ is alive reigning above with His saints. The culture of death is another deception of Satan. He uses "quality of life" as a justification for "euthanasia" and "euthanasia by omission." The deception is to escape old age or suffering under the banner of quality of life to kill oneself. The Devil knows that all those who engage in the culture of death either by committing suicide or any other form that destroys life are going straight to hell, into the Devil's domain. Why and how? God says that life is very sacred, so sacred that when one sinner repents and turns to God, there is always a big party and rejoicing in Heaven by the angels and the saints of God. Man does not create life, and must, therefore, not destroy life under the banner of any dogma. It is an act of rebellion and unbelief against God who advocates preservation of life because while there is life, there's always hope.

In science, the Law of Conservation of Mass states that "Mass or matter can be neither created nor destroyed." Therefore, any wish or wishes of man that oppose the guidelines of God must be discarded. Death was the end of everything, and the King and Lord of Death is Satan the Devil. But thanks be to God that through the death and cross of Jesus Christ, death has been conquered, and the keys of life and death are now held by Jesus Christ, the King of Kings, the Lord of Lords, and the Master of all Masters. Praise be to God.

Dear friend and reader, have you read the newspapers today, Have you listened to the television news today? Have you heard the CNN news? In the midst of all these bad news and problems of life, you can have peace today. Peace must be made with God first. Invite Jesus into your heart now. You will be "justified by his blood" and have peace with God. It is a special form of peace that human words cannot describe, and that is why St. Paul the apostle of Jesus wrote the epic line as "the Peace of God that passes all human understanding."

Congratulations for inviting Jesus into your heart. Welcome into the family of God.

A Sincere Look at Islam

M uslims are a distinct minority in the U.S., variously estimated at between three and six million adherents. There are over thirty million in Europe. Most of the 1.2 billion Muslims in the world are in Africa and Asia. They fall into two main groups, Sunni and Shiite, with conflicting claims to succession from the prophet Muhammad dating back to the seventh century.

Muhammad founded Islam on monotheism, taking as his antecedents Abraham, Moses, and Jesus. Thus, Islam claims the same origin as Judaism and Christianity, but Muhammad made the singular claim that he was the last prophet of God's word. Muhammad was a different kind of prophet in the sense that he was a temporal ruler as well, building his political base in Medina and then conquering the Arab city that had once rejected him, Mecca. After his death in June, 632, by traditional account, Arabs rapidly built an empire stretching from the gates of the Mediterranean to the far side of India, spreading Islam as they went.

The Islamic religion is a world-wide religion and reputed to be the fastest growing religion in the world today. The writer had a wonderful and loving uncle who was a dedicated Muslim. When the writer was between the ages of four and five, his uncle used to take him to the mosque, where he followed all the rituals of worship. As a child, the washing of the hands, feet and neck was regarded as a treat because it gave him the opportunity to play with water. Not that he knew what was going on, but it was fun to follow what the worshippers were doing and saying the "Recitation." Later on in life, it did not make any impact on the writer because of the attitude, foul language, actions, and lifestyles of those who profess Islamic beliefs in the environment. The writer had a relative who was a devout Muslim. He was a multi-talented man, a master-tailor and a great designer of men's suits. He designed the suits of the famous, and his name means "one who puts out fire by the recitation of Quran." However, he was a great womanizer, and the writer is convinced that it was the freedom given by Islam to marry at least four wives that lured him into Islam in the first place. As far as good works are concerned, he was a giant in giving. He gave when he did not even have. He was comical, hilarious, fun-loving, and a most generous man, loyal and extremely faithful to the family and friends alike. He had various vocabulary for the descriptions of the shapes and figures of women, referring to the backside of women as "basement," "platform," "stage," "rotunda," "flat," etc.

This is an area where the right type of education can be contrasted with the wrong type of education. What puzzled the writer was how this dedicated Muslim could live a lifestyle of sleeping with different women? When the writer was old enough and brave enough to ask that question, the answer given by the close relative shows the importance of receiving the right type of education and why education plays a significant role in the life of everyone. According to what he sincerely believed, he was satisfying and meeting the needs of those women and was actually doing them a favor and being a highly generous man, the word "resistance" or "control" were out of bounds in the school of generosity. Moreover, he added that according to Islam, "You are allowed to have as many women as you can afford, so long as you keep them happy." Being a very comical man, he said that the letter "me" in their language may mean 2, 3, 4, 6, 7, 8, 10, 12." Although four is the official number, he asked, "What does it matter if you can afford them and keep them happy?"

The response of the writer then was if what he said was true, how is it that at the beginning, Adam, the first man, was not given seven virgins or more but only one wife in the person of Eve? In the greatest wedding of man so far, and the most pompous, witnessed by all the angelic beings and animals and all the creations of God, Eve was married to Adam by God Himself, the Father of both. That was one of the queries of the writer, and the beginning of the "sincere look at Islam." Jesus Christ confirmed creation when He said that "in the beginning" God made them, male and female and commanded that man should not separate what God has joined together.

The fact of life is that one woman presents enough problems for her husband, and two, three, and four women will certainly multiply family problems and feuds, however good the management skills of the husband. There will be jealousy, anger, anguish, unhappiness, politics, palaver, plottings, perpetration, and precipitation of evil, a sense of insecurity among the wives; and the husband may have to resort to desperate means to assert his authority. The favorite wife becomes the target of hatred for others. Thanks to the British colonial masters of the time, the writer grew up mainly among Muslims and Christians. In point of fact, it was fifty-fifty for Christians and Muslims. At that time, the Muslims of the northern part of the country had a great reputation for kindness, contentment, and loyalty. Some of them migrated to the South and the capital city, which was mainly Christian with a large group of Muslims. The writer picked up some of the "terms" of Islam, such as "Salallam Moleku,""Aleku Sallam," the greeting of peace.

The writer got used to Ramadan, the celebration of Prophet Muhammad's receipt of the Quran. This is the process of fasting during daylight hours and feasting after dark. There are always interesting stories, but some of the comical ones were narrated by a friend of the writer to a group of his friends. During the Ramadan, some of the young ones at that time had a saying that "Only the foolish experience the pressure of fasting, but the wise know no such experience." This is the story of the young man. His father was a wealthy businessman, and, with his family, they celebrated Ramadan annually. Every morning this young man was at the early breakfast between 3:30 AM to 5:30 AM in the morning and fasted during daylight hours until sunset, between 6:00 PM and 7:00 PM with the entire family. His father was a school board member and one of the governors and trustees of the Muslim High School, open to Muslims and other faiths... Everyday at lunchtime the young professional teacher ordered his meal and ate it when he was supposed to be on the fast. He sat by the window side, and the building was such that passers-by could see what was going on inside. One day, the young teacher at lunchtime was enjoying his meal when his father's car pulled up and, on coming out of the car, he saw his son eating food. He was a wise man and instead of being furious at the beginning, he slipped into the lunchroom and made enquiries about the eating habits of his son. He was given the information that his son ordered his food daily during Ramadan. The young teacher saw his father when it was too late but, being a comical fellow, assuaged the anger of his father. The following morning, he joined the family again for the early breakfast and was chased out by his father. However, the food supply was so good that he went back and promised his father he would uphold the fast. He was eventually allowed back. The group of listeners asked him whether he kept his word, and the young man just giggled. That explained the saying that "The wise do not feel the pressure of the fast."

Let us now move from humor to reality and examine the claims of Islam. God our Maker encourages us to search out the scriptures and find out the truth ourselves. He is not a distant God but an ever present "Being," and a "very present help" in trouble. Therefore, all the queries, questions, and research work done are meant for the elucidation of the truth so that everyone may know the truth and be set free from the chains and fetters of ignorance and deceptions to embrace the light of joy, happiness, and peace.

Since Christianity is the world's largest religion and Islam is the second largest religion of about 1.2 to 1.5 billion people worldwide, we shall compare and contrast the two. Islam is the predominate religion in Arab countries, Pakistan, Indonesia, Bangladesh, Turkey, Malasia, Albania, many African nations, and some of the former Soviet Republics.

There are similarities and differences between Christianity and Islam. The Holy Bible grouped into the Old Testament, prior to Christ's earthly ministry, and the New Testament, including the four gospels and writings of the apostles in the first century of the church, make up the Holy Scriptures of the Christians.

The Quran or Koran (means "the recitation") is a collection of revelations supposedly given to Prophet Muhammad by the angel Gabriel. It is grouped into 114 chapters for each revelation and is the holy writings of Islam.

How did each book originate? St. Peter tells us that the Holy Bible came not "by the will of man, but holy men of God spoke as they were moved by the Holy Spirit." St. Peter also exalted "word of prophecy" and warned us to take heed. Fulfilled prophecy is a proof of inspiration. The Holy Bible forms one continuous story, the story of humanity in relation to God. It is a progressive unfolding of truth. The Bible hazards the most unlikely predictions concerning the future and, when the centuries have brought round the appointed time, records their fulfillment. From beginning to end, the Bible testifies to one redemption. From beginning to end, the Bible has one great theme, the person and work of the Christ. Finally, some forty-four writers in number writing through twenty centuries have produced a perfect harmony of doctrine in progressive unfolding. This is to every candid mind the unanswerable proof of the divine inspiration of the Holy Bible. We can, therefore, comprehend what St. Peter wrote in his letter that prophecy came not by the will of man but by holy men of God who spoke as they were moved by the Holy Spirit. Fulfilled prophecy is a proof of inspiration because the Holy Bible's predictions of future events were uttered so long before the events took place that no mere human wisdom or sagacity or foresight could have anticipated them; and these predictions are so detailed, minute, and specific as to exclude the possibility that they were simply fortunate guesses. Hundreds of predictions concerning Israel, the land of Canaan, Babylon, Assyria, Egypt, and numerous personages, so ancient, so singular, so seemingly improbable as well as detailed and definite that no mortal could have anticipated them, have been fulfilled by the elements and by men who were ignorant of them, or who utterly disbelieved them, or who struggled with frantic desperation to avoid their fulfillment. It is certain, therefore, that the scriptures which contain them are inspired. "Prophecy came not at any time by the will of man, but holy men of God spoke as they were moved by the Holy Spirit."

On the other hand, the Islamic Quran (Koran) is "the recitations" of collections of revelations supposedly given only to one man Muhammad by the angel Gabriel. In trying to find out the truth and explore the truth, certain fundamental questions come to mind but before these questions are asked, we need to have background knowledge and bear in mind that both Christianity and Islam agree on the existence of the devil.

Let us examine the personality of this being known by many names such as Satan, Lucifer, Beelzebub, Abaddon, Apollyon, Belial, Prince of the Demons, Prince of the Powers of the Air, Prince of this World. As serpent, he caused the fall of man. Lucifer or Satan who was the "son of the morning," appeared as an angel of light who said in his heart, "I will ascend into Heaven. I will exalt my throne above the stars of God. I will sit also upon the Mount of the Congregation, in the sides of the

North. I will ascend above the heights of the clouds. I will be like the Most High."

Therefore, we see from the beginning that the devil tries to copy God and all his actions are copy work of God but in a cunning and twisted way which appears genuine but is really rooted in deception and falsehood. The devil knows the Holy Scriptures very well as we observe in the temptations he put to Jesus in the wilderness. We can also see his manipulation of the Word of God by deliberately misquoting and omitting vital parts of the scriptures. When he asked Jesus to jump from the pinnacle of the temple if he is the son of God, we see two very important characteristics of the devil. Firstly, he knows that Jesus is the son of God, but he tries to create doubt in the mind of Jesus, hence he said "if you are the son of God" jump from the pinnacle. Secondly, he tried to persuade Jesus to jump quoting Psalm 91:11 as a guarantee of his safety. The truth is that the devil misquoted the scriptures by deliberately omitting the important phrase "in all thy ways" so as to suit his own purpose. Since that time, the devil has been misquoting the scriptures and has deceived many prophets. We have heard and read about false prophets who were deceived by the devil into thinking that they were speaking on God's behalf, when in fact, they were not sent by God.

With this background in view, let us ask ourselves certain fundamental questions of great importance. The first question is this: Is the God of the Bible, the God of Jesus Christ (because Jesus is the central figure in the Bible from Genesis to Revelation) the same God as Allah, the god of the Quran (Koran)? Let us not lose sight of the fact that there are many gods, many lords, many masters; and all these gods, lords, and masters have their own domain, empire, or kingdom as attested to by the Holy Scriptures of all religions.

We know already how the Holy Bible is written as we are told that holy men spoke as they were moved by the Holy Spirit. How did Quran come into existence? According to Prophet Muhammad, Quran, which is the bible of Islam, is presented as the final infallible witness of Allah. Before continuing, the writer wants all readers to know that everything being written, and questions being asked are meant only for educational purposes and the elucidation of the truth. Therefore, with malice towards none, with love towards all, the enquiries are rooted in sincerity and not an attempt to discredit anyone but rather to expose what seemingly appears to be the deceptions of Satan the evil one. Prophet Muhammad said the Quran is direct dictation from Allah through Gabriel. These revelations were not written by Prophet Muhammad himself but by scribes who wrote down his "revelations." Before going further, there are certain truths one must bear in mind. Prophet Muhammad's ancestry goes back to Ishmael, the first born of Abraham, but not the Son of Promise. Everyone should, therefore, love Ishmael and Prophet Muhammad because they are the children of Father Abraham and, therefore, they are our half-brothers. Whether half-brother or no half-brother, they are, in one word, our brothers and, therefore, it is incumbent upon us to love them. As brothers, if we see that they are heading in the wrong direction, it is our duty to point the right direction to them in love and without any acrimonious attitude. Let us remember that Ishmael and his brother Isaac buried Father Abraham in the cave of Machpelah in the field of Ephron, the son of Zohar the Hittite, east of Manre, the field which Abraham purchased from the Hittites. There, Abraham was buried with Sarah his wife (Genesis 25:9-10). The place today is known as the Tomb of the Patriarch in Hebron where the conflict for control of it still rages between the descendants of Isaac and Ishmael.

Let us now tackle important questions. Is Allah the god of Quran the same as Jehovah the God of the Holy Bible? We can honestly answer this by searching for the truth. If we think the answer is no because of various conflicts and contradictions, then the next reasonable question is which angel disguised as angel Gabriel when he appeared unto Prophet Muhammad? Did another angel disguised as angel Gabriel appear unto Prophet Muhammad claiming to be the archangel, Gabriel? Listen to the truthful declaration of Prophet Muhammad himself. He had his doubts whether these "revelations', were from angel Gabriel because of the way the revelations came about. They came in epileptic type seizures, and Prophet Muhammad admitted that he did not know whether the revelations were divine or demonic. His only wife at the time, Khadija, convinced him that the revelations were divine and from Allah. However, Prophet Muhammad himself admitted that some revelations were from Allah and some from Satan; therefore, Prophet

Muhammad withdrew some of his revelations saying that Satan had deceived him. Based upon this admission, we are compelled to ask the question — Could it then be true that it was Satan who disguised himself as angel Gabriel and gave those revelations which came in epileptic seizures? Could it be the case that Satan in trying to copy God engineered the whole concept of Allah, revealing that he had ninety-nine names? Could it be true that Islam, therefore, is a big project of Satan especially since one of the aims is to expand the territories ruled by Muslims at the expense of territories ruled by men? Is it to extend sovereign Muslim power? These are sincere questions being asked. They are not meant to offend anyone, but they are questions probing the truth. We know that Satan does not have original ideas of anything good except that he copies God in everything and tries to modify this in order to suit his purposes. He said, "I will ascend into Heaven. I will exalt my throne above the stars of God. I will sit upon the Mount of the Congregation, and in the sides of the North. I will ascend above the heights of the clouds. I will be like the Most High" (Isaiah 14: 13-14). Could it be, therefore, that Satan, looking at the progress of Christianity, engineered the concept of Islam as a copy of God's plan? When we look closely at Quran, it undoubtedly contains many modified Bible passages. It contains many statements that are internally contradictory or that are contrary to known facts. For example. it says that Abraham placed Ishmael on the altar to sacrifice, not Isaac, contrary to the writings of Moses in Genesis. Quran also claims that Ishmael is the Son of Promise, not Isaac, contrary to the writing of Moses. It says Saul was the leader of Gideon's army even though he was not yet born. It claims that Jesus was not crucified but it <u>appeared</u> that he was.

There are also internal contradictions in Quran:

1) Muslims are encouraged to fight to spread Islam, and, at the same time, there is the declaration that there is no compulsion in religion.

2) The number of angels who announced Jesus' coming to Mary varies from one to several.

3) Idolatry is listed as an unforgivable and a forgivable sin.

At this juncture, we must ask ourselves the question — Is the God of the Holy Bible the same god as Allah, the god of the Quran?

If you think or believe that they are the same, then we are compelled to make certain observations. The God of the Holy Bible is a God of progress, not a god of backwardness or retrogression. The Holy Bible is a progressive unfolding of truth. Nothing is told all at once and once for all. The Bible forms one continuous story, the story of humanity in relation to God. Without the possibility of collusion, often with centuries between, one writer of scripture takes up an earlier revelation, adds to it, lays down the pen, and, in due time, another man moved by the Holy Spirit, another, and another, add new details till the whole picture is complete. From Genesis, the Bible bears witness to one God. Wherever he speaks or acts, He is consistent with the total revelation concerning Him.

On the other hand, Allah the god of Islam revealed all the recitations to Muhammad the prophet, through angel Gabriel. This shows that the God of the Bible is not Allah, the god of the Quran. Secondly, the God of the Bible says, "Jesus Christ is the beloved son, in whom He is well-pleased." The god of Quran says Allah has no son, and that Jesus is not the son of God but just another prophet. Hence, we see that the God of the Bible is not the god of the Quran because the God of the Bible has a son, but Allah the god of Quran has no son. If the God of the Bible is Allah, He will not deny Jesus as His son in any genuine revelation to any prophet. Therefore, is it possible then that the god of Islam is one of the great deceptions of Satan the devil?

Let us consider the facts bearing in mind that the devil has nothing original in himself, but he copies God in all his actions. The greatest ambition of the devil is to be like the Most High God, and he led a rebellion in Heaven which precipitated his downfall. Since that time, the devil still holds the ambition to be like the Most High God by various acts. Could it be true that the devil manifesting himself as Allah tries once again to copy God?

Let us look at the creed of Islam. It says, "There is only one god Allah, and Muhammad is his prophet." This is the First Pillar of Islam. Could this be a copy of Judaism as found in Deuteronomy 6:4 - "Hear, O Israel, the Lord our God is one Lord." Could this be a copy of Judaism? It is claimed by Prophet Muhammad that Archangel Gabriel revealed all the recitations to him. Question — Is this the same archangel

Gabriel that was sent to Mary to deliver the message of the birth of Jesus Christ? Or is it another angel of the devil who assumed the name Gabriel and disguised as an angel of light to Prophet Muhammad? The reason for this line of questioning is that the words of angel Gabriel to Mary were, "Fear not, Mary, for you have found favor with God. And behold, you will conceive in your womb and bring forth a son and shall call his name Jesus. For He shall be great and shall be called the Son of the Highest (God), and the Lord God shall give unto Him, the throne of His Father David. And He shall reign over the House of Jacob forever, and of His kingdom there shall be no end. When Mary asked Angel Gabriel how shall this be since she knew no man, angel Gabriel said unto her, "The Holy Spirit shall come upon you and the power of the Highest shall overshadow you. Therefore, also, that Holy Thing which shall be born of you shall be called the Son of God." The puzzling question is how could this same angel Gabriel tell Prophet Muhammad that God has no son? Could it be possible that it was another angel who appeared unto Muhammad and disguised as an angel of light assuming the name of Archangel Gabriel? Surely, it could not be the same God who sent Archangel Gabriel to announce the coming of His son that sent the same archangel Gabriel to reveal that He has no son! This tends to show that Allah the god of the Muslims is not the God of Jesus Christ.

There are so many references in the Bible that identify Jesus as the Son of God. Isaiah 9:6 says, "For unto us a child is born, unto us a son is given, and the government shall be upon His shoulder, and His name shall be called Wonderful, Counselor, the Mighty God, the Everlasting Father, the Prince of Peace."

Jesus is the Prince of Peace according to the scriptures, and by His sacrifice He made peace between God and man. God is a God of progress who changed the old covenant for a new covenant with His people. As the writer to the Hebrews puts it, if the first covenant had been faultless, then should no place have been sought for the second. But God put away the old covenant and gave a new covenant which is one of the significant covenants of scripture and is remarkably full. The new covenant, the last of the eight great covenants of scripture, is better than the Mosaic covenant, not morally, but efficaciously.

1) It is established upon "better" (i.e., unconditional) promises. In the Mosaic covenant, God said, "If you will..." In the new covenant, He says, "1 will..."

2) Under the Mosaic covenant, obedience sprang from fear. Under the new, it issues from a willing heart and mind.

3) The new covenant secures the personal revelation of the Lord to every believer. This is one of the cogent reasons Allah the god of Islam is not the Yahweh or Jehovah of the Lord Jesus Christ.

4) The new covenant assures the complete oblivion of sins.

5) It rests upon accomplished redemption.

A Muslim proselyte once told a friend of the writer that everyone is born a Muslim. This is absolutely incorrect, not true but the other way round. Everyone is born a "redeemable Christian." He is born under the condemnation of sin in the DNA that he inherited from his parents but is redeemable because "Before the foundation of the world, Jesus Christ was slain for the redemption of man and had spiritually sustained the five wounds that were later evident at the cross. This is because Christ has already been slain before the foundation. of the world, that is before man was created, Jesus Christ already redeemed man. Hence two and three makes up the five wounds on the cross. The second interpretation of two and three is 23 pairs of chromosomes in every human being, the Code of Ownership of Man by God through Jesus Christ. This means that everyone is born a redeemable Christian. Everyone has the potential to be redeemed if he or she makes the choice and invites Jesus Christ to come in and change the gene-carrying sin of rebellion and disobedience. This is the scientific explanation of "being born again" from sin to righteousness, from rebellion to obedience through love, and from spiritual death to spiritual life.

To repeat this important concept, figure 2 and 3 or 23 pairs of chromosomes is the mark or code of Jesus in every human being and also corresponds to the five wounds of Jesus on the cross. This is one of the reasons "every knee shall bow and confess that Jesus is Lord of all, King of Kings, and Lord of Lords." The scientists think figure 23 pairs of chromosomes is meaningless, but that is not so. It is the code they do not know about and hence discard as meaningless, but God is wisdom and there is no "meaningless" with Him.

Another indisputable mark of Jesus in every human being is the figure 8 pattern of the human circulatory system, testifying that Jesus in the will of the Father is the sole owner of every human being who comes to Him by faith. Dear Reader, would you not be excited to know that you can find out the truth yourself so that your faith or religion is not standing in the wisdom of men, in the rather sounding glamorous speculation of men, but in the power, might, and wisdom of the Holy Spirit of God? You, too, can be like a scientist repeating successful experiments for validation. Your very thoughts are naked before God and if you have an open mind genuinely desirous of the truth, you will obtain remarkable results. Remember the woman, with the blood disease that Jesus healed. She said within herself, "If I could but touch the hem of His garment, I know I will be healed." She touched the hem of the garment of Jesus, and she was healed. This confirms what Psalm 139 says that God knows all our thoughts. Therefore, you, too, can experience the same mighty power of God by saying the following prayer: "Jesus, come into my heart now Root out all evil from within me. Wash me by your precious blood and fill me with your Holy Spirit." If you say those words sincerely in faith and by faith, you will be a new person with a new outlook in life. If you experience peace within and joy indescribable, these are signs of your new birth in Christ Jesus. These signs should encourage you that your faith is valid because of the existence of God.

Let us go back to our comparison of Islam, Judaism, and Christianity. Let us look at the Second Pillar of Islam which is called "Salat" or "Prayer." It is the basic tenet of Islam and ultimate worship for the Muslims. The number of times of praying in a day lends credence to the suggestion that Islam is a copy of the early Christian habits of prayer. It is said that when Prophet Muhammad was carried by the angel to the throne of Allah, he was given the duty of prayer 40 times a day. It is claimed that on his way from the throne of Allah, he met Moses who told him that 40 times is very burdensome, and he should go back for reduction. He went back, and it was reduced, and, on his return, he met Moses again who told him that the new number was still high and burdensome and that he should go back for more reduction. The process of going back to Allah's throne was repeated a number of times until the number was finally reduced to five times. Is this a copy of the early Christian habits of prayer? The early Christians performed major prayer assignments five times a day. The first is 6:00 AM because of the belief most probably carried forward from Judaism that at 6:00 AM, there are angels performing various functions and services to man for all purposes of life. The second time of prayer was at 9:00 AM when the angels distributing spiritual gifts take over for those on duty from 6:00 AM. The third time of prayer was 12:00 noon when another set of angels take over duty. These angels help people to be victorious over all the daily problems of life, and they are believed to be under the generalship of Archangel Michael. The fourth time of prayer was at 3:00 PM when another set of angels take over duty. These angels perform healing acts to those praying or asking for various forms of healing. They are believed to be under the command of Archangel Raphael.

The fifth time of prayer is at 6:00 PM when angels meeting all needs of life go on duty. These constituted the five times of praying exercises by the early Christian. In many parts of the world today some Christians still follow the apostolic ways of praying five times a day although the number of times should actually be limitless for all believing Christians. We are exhorted to pray without ceasing and we should pray every hour or every minute of the day. Then we become supermen of God in Christ Jesus.

We see, therefore, how the early Christian believers operated. The culture at the time was "early to bed and early to rise" so that the routine of devotional prayer could be followed. We, therefore, establish similarity in the prayer habits of five times a day of the early Christians and five times a day for the Muslims.

The Quran contains many statements that are internally contradictory or that are contrary to known facts. For example, Muslims believe Abraham was called to sacrifice Ishmael rather than Isaac and claim that God's covenant is with Ishmael. However, the facts tell a different story. The Lord God of the Hebrews made eight covenants:

1) The Edenic Covenant (Genesis 2:16) conditions the life of man is innocence,

2) The Adamic Covenant (Genesis 3:15) conditions the life of fallen man and gives promise of a redeemer. (Prophet Muhammad is not the redeemer),

3) The Noahic Covenant (Genesis 9:16) establishes the principle of human government,

4) The Abrahamic Covenant (Genesis 12:2) founds the Nation of Israel (not the Nation of Islam) and confirms with specific additions the Adamic promise of redemption,

5) The Mosaic Covenant (Exodus 19:5) condemns all men (as confirmed by Romans 3:23, "for all have sinned,"

6) The Palestinian Covenant (Deuteronomy 30:3) secures the final restoration and conversion of Israel (not Ishmael),

7) The David Covenant (2 Samuel 7:16) establishes the perpetuity of the Davidic family (fulfilled in Christ, Matthew 1:1, Luke 1:31-33, Romans 1:3) and of the Davidic Kingdom over Israel and over the whole earth to be fulfilled in and by Christ (not Prophet Muhammad) (2 Samuel 7:8-17, Zechariah 12:8, Luke 1:31-33, Acts 5:14-17, 1 Corinthians 15:24), and finally

8) The New Covenant (Hebrews 8:8) rests upon the sacrifice of Christ and secures eternal blessedness under the Abrahamic Covenant of all who believe. It is absolutely unconditional and since no responsibility is by it committed to man, it is final and irreversible. Do not let Satan deceive you any longer. Islam or Muhammadanism does not come under the covenants.

Modern Arabs trace their ancestry to Shem, oldest son of Noah, from whom Abraham descended, who fathered Ishmael, his firstborn by Hagar, the Egyptian lady. Hagar was driven out of Abraham's home through the instructions of Sarah, the legitimate wife of Abraham. How did Ishmael come into the picture?

God made a promise to Abraham and Sarah that their seed will be as countless as the stars. Abraham believed God, and it was counted to him for righteousness. However, after ten years elapsed and Sarah had not yet conceived, the old crafty devil put seeds of doubt into Sarah's mind. The devil did not go to Abraham because he knew his faith was solid as a rock, but he went to Sarah. He said to Sarah, "Do you not think that ten years is enough time for God to give you a child? Be realistic. You are too old now to conceive because you are past the age of childbearing. You better do something about it if you truly love Abraham your husband." It was the devil who made the suggestion to Sarah to give Hagar her maid to Abraham. Dear Reader, do you see the strategy of the devil? It was not because the devil cared about Sarah but because he saw an avenue to derail God's plan. He appeared sympathetic to Sarah and presented what looked to Sarah as the solution to her problem but in fact was the seed of enmity and hatred between the seed of Hagar (Ishmael) and the seed of Sarah (Jesus Christ).

Sarah, therefore, persuaded her husband Abraham to take Hagar her maid and "Maybe she might obtain children by her." Can you see the heart of true love and sincerity of Sarah for her husband Abraham? Abraham listened to her petition and, in order to please her, he obeyed Sarah. Do you not see a parallel in the role of Eve in persuading Adam against the guidelines of God?

The strategy of the devil has not changed. He has been using women right through the ages to cause the downfall of man. Abraham went in unto Hagar, and she conceived. Abraham was eight-four years old when Hagar bore Ishmael to him. However, when Abraham was ninety-nine years old, God appeared unto him and reiterated His promise of the legitimate son. The Holy Scripture records in Genesis 17:17 that "Abraham fell upon his face and laughed and said in his heart, shall a child be born unto him who is a hundred years old? And shall Sarah that is ninety years old, bear?" And Abraham said unto God, "Oh, that Ishmael might live before Thee." He thought the covenant would be between him and Ishmael who at that time was about sixteen years old. However, God said, "Sarah, thy wife, shall bear thee a son indeed, and thou shalt call his name Isaac, and I will establish my covenant with him for an everlasting covenant, and with his seed after him" (Genesis 17:19). We see here that the covenant is between God, Abraham, and Isaac, and not with Ishmael.

Nevertheless, God says in Genesis 17:20, "And as for Ishmael, I have heard your plea. Behold I have blessed him and will make him fruitful and will multiply him exceedingly. Twelve princes shall he beget, and I will make him a great nation" (the Arabs).

Genesis 17:21 says, "But my covenant will I establish with Isaac, whom Sarah shall bear unto thee at this set time in the next year." The word of God came to pass, and Isaac was born. There are two notable miracles here. Abraham was a hundred years old when Isaac was born unto him. The second miracle was Sarah's giving birth to Isaac at nine-one years old. Surely, nothing is too hard for the Lord our God.

While Christianity holds the Holy Bible as the "divinely inspired, inerrant (without error), unchanging Word of God, Islam and Muslims believe in the Law of Moses (first 5 books of the Bible), Psalms of David, and the Injil (Gospel of Jesus Christ). However, Muslims believe these books of the Bible are superceded by "revelations" given to Muhammad and claim that the Bible used by Christians and Jews (Old Testament) is a distorted version of the Bible. Wherever the Bible contradicts the teaching of Islam, the Bible is viewed as incorrect. There is a problem here because any open-hearted person who reads the Holy Bible from Genesis to Revelation will notice perfect harmony and the consistency of God throughout and all the time. The Quran contains three provisions for "abrogation," an annulment or destruction of previous revelations, meaning that God's Word can be changed at its choosing and that God's divine revelation can be inconsistent and subject to change. If we examine the facts, we see that the claims of Islam do not fit the facts. How is it possible that God, who is the God of progress who changed the Old Testament covenant to the New Testament covenant because the blood of bulls and of goats could not take away sins and gave His son Jesus as the final sacrifice, could then revert to the slaughter of bulls and goats? It is the unacceptable deceit of the devil. Quran acknowledges that Jesus performed miracles and was the Messiah, born of a virgin, but says He did not die on the cross. Muslim traditions believe he was miraculously delivered from death, being taken bodily into Heaven without dying.

To say that Jesus did not die on the cross is the greatest human deception of the devil since the fall of Adam. The glorious truth is that Jesus is the Lamb of God who shed His blood for the remission of sins of mankind, for without the blood there is no remission of sins. If Jesus did not die on the cross, then Christianity is a sham, and Christians are the most pitiable of all people. But the triumphant and glorious truth is that Jesus did die on the cross and by His precious blood we have forgiveness of our sins, we have salvation from death, we have free access to God, we are washed, justified, sanctified, and sealed unto eternity by the Holy Spirit of Jesus sent down by the Father since the day of Pentecost.

As recorded in Isaiah 53:3-5, Jesus "is despised and rejected of men, a man of sorrows and acquainted with grief...Surely Jesus bore our griefs and carried our sorrows. But [Jesus] was wounded for our transgressions; He was bruised for our iniquities. The chastisement for our peace was upon Him, and with His stripes we are healed."

Blood is life, and the shedding of the blood of Jesus gives a new life to all believers. This is why anyone in Jesus Christ who has been born again is a new creature. Moreover, there were eye-witnesses to the death of Jesus on the cross: his mother, disciples, Roman soldiers, high priests of Judaism who were gloating, and the Roman citizens as well as the two thieves who were crucified along with Jesus. Jesus received five wounds on the cross with His blood spilling onto the ground as an eternal sacrifice for the redemption of man.

The Roman centurion who was an eye witness of the crucifixion confessed that "Surely Jesus is the Son of God." Before Jesus died, He suffered agony on the cross, and in Matthew 27:46, we read that Jesus cried with a loud voice, saying, "Eli, Eli, Lama Sabachtani? My God, my God why hast Thou forsaken me?" Jesus was forsaken on the cross because God cannot look upon sin. Jesus died on the cross. He was not miraculously delivered from death nor bodily taken into Heaven. When Jesus uttered His last words, "It is finished" before he died, He sealed the redemption of man. It is recorded by eye-witnesses that the veil of the temple in the Holy of Holies was split and torn apart, giving all believers in Christ free access to God in the Holy of Holies.

If Jesus did not die on the cross, then there was no resurrection; and if there is no resurrection, then Christianity is false. But is it? The devil operating sleekly through Islam wants the world to believe that all these documented events did not happen because of "questionable revelations" underwritten by him that Jesus was bodily taken into Heaven without dying. This is surely one of the revelations that Prophet Muhammad himself questioned as being from the devil. How do we know this? Right from the day of resurrection, the devil has been raising up people and stirring them up to disbelieve and discredit the resurrection. The Roman soldiers who guarded the sepulcher that was sealed by a hefty stone reported all the things they saw to the chief priests. The chief priests with the elders bribed the Roman soldiers with fortunes of money to tell lies that the disciples came by night and stole Him away while they slept. They promised to use all their available resources and influence to secure and protect them from the governor.

History records that the Roman soldiers took the money and did as they were taught, but it was an open secret to the public at that time that they were not telling the truth. The resurrection story was hard for certain people to accept. Even Thomas, one of the disciples of Jesus, when he was told by his friends and other colleagues that Jesus had arisen from the dead said, "Except I shall see in His hands the print of the nails and put my finger into the print of the nails and thrust my hand into his side, I will not believe." We are told that the next time Jesus appeared to the disciples, Jesus asked Thomas to thrust his hand into his side before Thomas believed.

The resurrection of Jesus Christ is the heart of the Christian message. The burial of Jesus confirms evidence of his death; and the fact that He was seen alive by His disciples, the high priests, friends, foes, relatives, and, on one occasion, by thousands of believers is proof of His resurrection. The resurrection transformed the lives of the apostles and the relatives of Jesus. It was the resurrection that convinced the brothers of Jesus that He is the Messiah. During Christ's earthly ministry, and prior to the resurrection, all his brothers did not believe in Him. It was after the resurrection that James, Jude, and the other brothers believed in Jesus, with James and Jude becoming pillars in the church and each credited with important books in the New Testament Bible.

The importance and significance is not only that in Christ Jesus all believers shall gain eternal life, but it signifies the restoration of man to kingship lost by Adam

Importance of Women in the Lives of Men

In the wisdom of God, Mary Magdalene, a woman, was the first person to whom the Lord Jesus revealed His identity after the resurrection. One of the reasons was the sincerity of her heart for the cause of Christ's kingdom, but the main reason was the rectification of the fall of the first man through Eve, a woman, by Mary Magdalene, a woman of faith. In the scenario of the fall of king and prophet Adam engineered by the devil, but executed through Eve, who appeared to be a faithless woman in trusting the devil instead of trusting God, God used Mary Magdalene, a woman of faith in God, who gladly and joyfully saw the glory of God in the appearance of the resurrected Jesus Christ. Therefore, Mary Magdalene carried the good news of the resurrection of the Lord Jesus to the other disciples of Jesus. The news that the Lord Jesus Christ, the second Adam, has restored the first and fallen Adam to kingship and is co-heir with the Lord Jesus Christ King of Kings, Lord of Lords, the Master of all Masters and savior of the entire world, has accomplished the unimaginable.

Throughout history, God has used women in the lives of men. God made Miriam, the sister of Aaron and Moses, a prophetess, and most probably the first minister of music, who took timbrel in her hand and led all the Israelite women dancing and singing praises to the Lord after God destroyed the military might of the Egyptians in the Red Sea.

God raised up Deborah as a prophetess. She was the wife of Lapidoth and became a judge over the nation of Israel. In short, she was made the leader or prime minister of the nation by God. She and Barak led the children of Israel to a decisive military victory over Sisera, the military commander of the Canaanites.

God used Huldah, the prophetess and wife of Shallum in delivering important messages and guidance to Josiah, King of Judah, and her words ignited fire in the heart of Josiah which led to a great revival and reformation in the days of King Josiah.

God used Esther, chosen as queen of Persia, to deliver the Jews from complete annihilation, and her work of deliverance is still commemorated annually by the Jews all over the world.

Women formed the backbone of the support team of the ministry of our Lord Jesus Christ. We see the consistency and wisdom of God in all His actions. Since it was Eve, the first woman, who gave Adam the "counterfeit good news" of how they can be like God knowing good from evil, it was not surprising that it was through another woman Mary Magdalene who first saw the Lord Jesus Christ after

His resurrection from the dead and took the "real good news" to the disciples and believers.

Let us now give a sincere look at Islam and the role of women in Islam in a nutshell. It is claimed that Islam came into existence because of the role of Khadija, the wife of Prophet Muhammad. When the prophet doubted the revelations because of the way in which he had received them, by seizures, having second thoughts that the devil may be behind it all, it was Khadija who encouraged the prophet and convinced him that the revelations were divine from Allah. So, without the influence of Khadija on Prophet Muhammad, Islam could not have come into existence.

There are fundamental differences between Christianity and Islam. One of the pivotal differences between Christianity and Islam is that the God of Jesus Christ is the God of Peace who did not allow King David to build the temple because he was a man of war and had shed too much blood. Therefore, his son Solomon built the temple. Jesus taught peace and gave the commandment to all Christian believers to love their enemies and do good to those who oppress them or hate them. He set an everlasting example on the cross. When all his enemies and distractors were mocking him, he prayed for them saying, "Father, forgive them for they do not know what they are doing." This is a veritable confirmation that ignorance is the malady of man.

In Islam, on the other hand, according to Quran, Allah has no regard for blood, and Muhammad taught Jihad as a means to expand Islam. The Christians, too, were deceived by the devil in the "Christian Jihad" from 1095 to about 1291. The Christian crusaders were wrong because they acted contrary to the teaching of the Lord, Master, and Savior Jesus Christ. The teachings of Jesus are explicit. "Love your enemies, bless them that curse you, do good to them that hate you, and pray for them who despitefully use you and persecute you. That ye may be sons (not slaves) of your Father, who is in Heaven, who maketh His sun to rise on the evil and on the good and sendeth rain to the just and the unjust" (Matthew 5:44-45). As we have read earlier, Jesus did not only teach peace, but He set the example on the cross when He prayed for His enemies. The apostles and disciples of Jesus became martyrs without retaliation. The Great Commission given by Jesus to

His disciples and followers is to go to all nations and teach them all things He commanded them, one of which is to love one another, including their enemies.

There is no compulsion in proclaiming Christ. Everyone is free to accept or reject the Good News without force or violence, but there are consequences for our choices. Those that receive the good news of Jesus, and His resurrection will have eternal life, and those that reject the good news, eternal damnation. The line is clear, and there is no gray area or middle lane. It is either obedience to the truth for life eternal or disobedience to the truth for eternal damnation.

On the other hand, in Islam, at the beginning, there was instant judgment. The choice was Islam or your head with a flashing sword. So we see another fundamental difference between Christianity and Islam. Jesus says, "Love your enemies." Prophet Muhammad says, "Kill the infidels."

Certain thinkers perceive that one of the great deceptions of Satan to Prophet Muhammad is the Jihad (Holy Way). They ponder the questions:

1) Is the Jihad that Quran teaches an internal struggle?

2) Or is it a physical conflict between Muslims and non-Muslims?

3) Is the Quran's call to Jihad only for defense?

Some of these thinkers argue that it is in Jihad that we see the true colors of Satan flying. Jihad, if it is a physical conflict between Muslims and non-Muslims is unquestionably one of the pivotal differences between Christianity and Islam. The opinion of the writer is that anyone who thinks he or she is fighting for God by killing others is deceived because God does not need any man or person to fight for Him. If God wants to fight against man, He can use winds, storms, hurricanes, flooding by water, rain, ants, locusts, arid what man regards as insignificant to fight against him. The two recent deadly hurricanes Katrina and Rita that hit America is a reminder to all. Is God calling America back to holiness? Is God speaking to America through these hurricanes? From whatever angle we look at it, "good" has come out of the hurricanes. We see the out outpouring of love and the triumph of love over all barriers. We see the mercies of God in judgment but above all the faithfulness of God hovering over the nation.

Therefore, let believers and non-believers alike learn a great lesson that power belongs to God, and He rules His universe. Is the purpose of Jihad engineered by the devil? Is Jihad intended to spread Islamic faith or to extend sovereign Muslim power with the eventual goal of achieving Muslim dominion over the entire globe? Is this reminiscent of the World Empire that Satan the devil offered to Jesus but was rejected by Jesus during the temptation of Jesus by the devil? World Empire is the ambition of Satan. Is it reflected in one of the revelations to Prophet Muhammad?

This chapter has given us a sincere look at Islam and contrasted it with Christianity. One of the carrots dangled to young people of Muslim faith is the inheritance of seven virgins or twelve virgins or seventy-two virgins on arrival in Paradise and the erroneous belief that the killing of non-believers labeled "infidels" ensures instant ticket to Paradise. This shows parallelism with the old concept of the Egyptian kings whereby all their earthly treasures were buried with them with the belief of living pleasurable lives in the life after. This presents Islam as a religion of the flesh if Jihadians expect twelve virgins in Paradise. This also reveals one of the fundamental differences between Christianity and Islam. In Christianity, the Lord Jesus Christ tells us that in Heaven, women are not given in marriage, but they are as angels before God. Christianity, in contrast, is a religion of the Holy Spirit because of the personal relationship between the believer and Jesus Christ through the Holy Spirit of God. Whereas the accelerated attainment to Paradise in Islam is by Jihad, the killing of innocent people dubbed as infidels (a complete abrogation and annulment of a God with principle), the attainment to Christian Paradise is by faith in Jesus Christ through holiness and righteousness. This is accomplished by being born again by the Holy Spirit of God and Christ. Also, the Christians are taught that flesh and blood cannot inherit the Kingdom of God which is the Kingdom of Peace, Righteousness, and Joy in the Holy Spirit. Through the declaration

of Jesus Christ, we know that God is a spirit, and they that worship Him must worship Him in spirit and in truth (John 4:24).

We know from the Holy Scriptures that the one and only true God places emphasis on the sanctity of life and teaches us the importance of one life or soul when the good shepherd secured the ninety-nine sheep and went after the lost one. He found the lost one and rejoiced exceedingly. The sanctity of life is the first and most important duty God grants to government. The true God hates all workers of iniquity (Psalm 5). He abhors the bloody and deceitful man. If you are a Muslim and you do not believe what you have just read, please go to Sura, Chapter 10:94. It refers you back to the Book (the five books of Moses, the Psalms, and the Gospels).

Another fundamental difference between Christianity and Islam is "blood tissue." Prophet Muhammad said that blood is unimportant to Allah and taught the shedding of innocent blood for the sake of Allah; but the God of truth, the Lord God of the Hebrews, the God of Jesus Christ, says that blood is the life, and the shedding of the blood of Jesus gives a new life to anyone who believes in Jesus. The blood is so important and significant that the Word of God says, "Without shedding of blood, there is no remission of sins" (Hebrews 9:22).

The most disturbing factor is that many innocent young Muslims acting out of their belief of instant Paradise have become suicide bombers and have gone straight to Hell and not Paradise because of the deception of Satan. How do we know this? The Holy Scriptures tell us that the true God has no dealings with evil, wickedness, or murder. He forbade the sacrifice of children to so-called "gods." He is the God of Peace. Anything that has to do with evil, wickedness, blood shedding of the innocent, murder in any shape or form, death, are all of Satan the devil, the Prince of the Culture of Death.

The Quran, the holy book of Islam, confirms that Jesus performed miracles, but that Muhammad did not perform any miracle. It also states that Muhammad sinned and needed forgiveness (Sura 40:55). But Jesus was sinless (Sura 3:46).

Finally, Islam is a works religion besides being a religion of the flesh. There is no guarantee of Paradise unless one is a martyr in Jihad. One's good works are put on one side of the scale and his bad works on the other side. Paradise is determined by how the scales tip, and no one knows until he dies.

On the other hand, Christianity is the religion of faith, and Hebrews 11:6 tells us that "Without faith, it is impossible to please God for he cometh to God must believe that He is, and He is a rewarder of them that diligently seek Him." In Islam, Paradise is uncertain until you die. Christianity gives the assurance of certainty and surety of eternal life in Christ Jesus because of the resurrected power of Jesus. As a born-again believer in Jesus, you are justified before God, you are sanctified, you are baptized by the Holy Spirit of Jesus, you are sealed (guaranteed) unto eternity by the Holy Spirit of God, and you have perfect peace with God.

What is your choice?

You have freedom to choose. Have you made up your mind yet? Would you like to hear the candid words of the Prophet Muhammad? Prophet Muhammad said, "I do not know what Allah will do with me." Therefore, in Islam the question of Paradise is one of probability, doubt and uncertainty. Paradise (Muslim heaven) will be an earthly place of gluttony and fleshly gratification. In contrast, Christianity teaches that the Kingdom of God is not food and drink but righteousness, peace, and joy in the Holy Spirit. In 1 Corinthians 6:9-11, the Holy Bible says, "Know ye not that the unrighteous shall not inherit the Kingdom of God? Be not deceived. Neither fornicators, nor idolaters, nor adulterers, nor effeminate, nor abusers of themselves with mankind, nor thieves, nor covetous, nor drunkards, nor revilers, nor extortioners, shall inherit the Kingdom of God." And such were some of us. But we are washed; we are sanctified in the name of the Lord Jesus and by the Spirit of our God. St. Paul the apostle tells us in Titus 1:11-14 that "The grace of God that brings salvation has appeared to all men," teaching us that denying ungodliness and worldly lusts, we should live soberly, righteously, and godly in this present age, looking for that blessed hope and the glorious appearing of the great God and our Savior Jesus Christ who gave Himself for us that He might redeem us from all iniquity and purify unto Himself a people of His own, zealous of good works.

My Dear Reader, what is your choice? Certainty of eternal life or doubt of eternal life? For certainty of eternal life, use this simple prayer: "Lord Jesus, wash me by your precious blood. Root out all evil and wickedness from within me. Set your throne of holiness and righteousness in me and make me a new creature by your Holy Spirit. Amen"

Welcome into the family of God. Hallelujah.

Why I Believe
In God, Jesus Christ and
the Holy Spirit

The Faithful Witness
A Special Appeal
to all Atheists, Agnostics, and Apologetics in Particular,

And all People in General

This chapter in a way is the most difficult chapter to write but the most joyful to narrate. It is the most difficult chapter to write because it may be politically incorrect, goes against the norm of unbelief, exposes the writer to various vindictive attacks and probably being labeled a "Wacko" for daring to fish in troubled waters. Nevertheless, it is a joy to write a testimony of the truth so that there is no excuse for anyone not being born again into the glorious family of God. For this reason, this chapter is dedicated to all atheists, agnostics, and apologetics in particular, and to all people in general.

This report is the true testimony of a faithful servant of God writing an eye-witness account of the various revelations and visions of God our Heavenly Father, purely and solely for all atheists, agnostics, apologetics in particular, for the benefits and encouragements of all people of every tribe, race, color, or creed in every part of this planet earth. The scripture says, "Our faith is valid because of the existence of God who can make the dead live and speak His words to those not yet born."

The purpose of this report, therefore, is to confirm the existence of God as written in the Holy Scriptures because this God has appeared to the writer and taught him various lessons that are recorded in this chapter. This captivating chapter is the story of an eye-witness account of the revelations and visions of God to an individual in the twentieth and twenty-first centuries. The visions and revelations started in the twentieth century when the writer was only four years old.

These visions and revelations are being shared with all people so that everyone who wants to know the absolute truth can come into the knowledge of the truth with probably similar experiences and in so doing come to know the one and only true God, the Blessed Father of our Lord and Savior Jesus Christ.

It is all praise and thanks to God who grants permission to share all the revelations and visions with all people as a witness so that no one can give an excuse of not hearing the confirmation of the existence of God and the good news of eternal life and felicity, available for all who believe in Jesus Christ as the only true and sure way back to God. It is not the wish of God that any should perish, and the testimony in these visions and revelations may be the last opportunity for many before they pass away and miss eternal life.

At this point, let us recall the eye-witness account of the Lord Jesus Christ in the story about the rich man, the beggar Lazarus, and Father Abraham in Heaven. Jesus gave an eye-witness account of a certain rich man who was clothed in purple and fine linen and fared sumptuously every day. And there was a certain beggar named Lazarus who lay at his gate full of sores and desiring to be fed with the crumbs which fell from the rich man's table. Moreover, the dogs came and licked his sores. And it came to pass that the beggar died and was carried by the angels into Abraham's bosom. The rich man also died and was buried. In Hades, the rich man lifted up his eyes, being in torment, and saw Abraham afar off and Lazarus in his bosom. And he cried and said, "Father Abraham, have mercy on me and send Lazarus that he may dip the tip of his finger in water and cool my tongue for I am tormented in this flame." But Abraham said, "Sir, remember that in your lifetime, you received your good things and likewise Lazarus, evil things, but now he is comforted and you are tormented. And besides all this, between us and you, there is a great gulf fixed, so that they who would pass from here that to you cannot, neither can they pass to us, that would come from thee." Then he said, "I pray thee, therefore, Father Abraham, that you send someone to my father's house for I have five brothers that they may testify unto them." Abraham said unto him, "They have Moses and the prophets. Let them hear them." And he said, "Nay, Father Abraham, but if one went unto them from the dead, they would repent." And he said unto him, "If they hear not Moses and the prophets, neither will they be persuaded, though one rose from the dead." That was the eye-witness account as told by the Lord Jesus Christ to his audience.

Today we see the truth of the declaration of Father Abraham that if the brothers could not believe Moses and the prophets neither will they be persuaded though one rose from the dead. How true this is today. Jesus Christ rose from the dead, appeared to so many people, and before His ascension, gave the Great Commission to His disciples. "Go ye, therefore, and teach all nations baptizing them in the name of the Father and the Son and of the Holy Spirit. Teaching them to observe all things that I commanded you and lo, I am with you always even unto the end of time."

One person has arisen from the dead and tells us the good news of freedom from the captivity of Satan to eternal life and felicity, but how many have believed on Him who rose from the dead to give us hope? My Dear Readers, you see why Father Abraham is right. If one rose up from the dead and warned them about Hell and eternal damnation, they would not believe because they are deceived by Satan that the God of Love would not do that. They have their own imaginations about God which are deceptions of Satan. Friends, there is no more excuse for anyone to reject the good news of Jesus Christ. The writer, therefore, is sharing his visions and revelations to all people so that there is no excuse for atheists, agnostics, apologetics, and unbelievers to turn their backs against God. God is still calling them by this testimony because it is not His wish that any should perish.

The visions and revelations of God to the writer when he was four years old. He lived with his family in a duplex family house, and one day his mother made a very tasty beef stew. The writer decided to have more, not by asking or requesting but by unacceptable means. The front part of the duplex house was the living part of the house while the back part was the pantry and kitchen. While the parents were in the front part of the house in the evening around 7:00 PM, the writer sneaked out into the kitchen and pantry, locked the door, and began without permission to eat beef from the pot. Before hearing the end of the story, please take note of very important facts. The first fact is that the person concerned was only four years old, an age many people call "age of innocence," but the fact is that before that age the genes of sin, disobedience, rebellion, inherited from parents, are already in operation. At the age of four, he decided from his heart that he would obtain materials in an incorrect and improper manner. He locked the door of the kitchen and pantry, so he knew at that age without anyone instructing him that what he was about to do was wrong. It was out of his heart that he planned to have his own way and do what was pleasing to him without thinking of his parents and others. Is this not what people do today? People are so infected with the disease of self and selfishness that they do whatever they want to do regardless of the consequences to others. So, what happened was that, even at the age of four, as soon as the writer put the beef into his mouth and finished eating, the vision of God in the likeness of a Heavenly Father appeared unto him and asked him a question, "Do you not know what you are doing? You are stealing and it is wrong to steal. Do not do it again." And the vision disappeared. The writer cannot remember whether he felt any guilt. However, he remembers very well what was uppermost in his heart. He determined in his heart that he would from that time on follow the instructions of the Heavenly Father and would not participate again in such an unacceptable behavior. He did not tell his parents about the vision of God but kept it within himself.

Friends, atheists, agnostics, apologetics, unbelievers, that testimony is for you. There is a God in Heaven, and He is our Heavenly Father, and He cares about our remotest activity because He wants the best for us in every department of our lives. There is no excuse for you now to doubt the existence of this God of Love, and He will reveal Himself to you when and if you seek Him with earnestness of mind and sincerity. That testimony is not a fluke but the beginning of various revelations and visions of God Himself to the writer.

Testimony No. 2 — God as Protector and Guide

The next narrative is to confirm that God is our Protector and Guide in life as we yield and surrender ourselves to Him. Just a few months after the pantry and kitchen revelation and at almost five years old, there was a big family wedding and brass bands with guests and family members dancing round the city within a radius of three to five miles. The writer was assigned to a maid for protection and care while everybody danced. As a child of about five, the writer was soon fed up with all the festivities going on. He was in the midst of a large crowd in the procession and parade with music, dancing, and a lot of noise. The writer decided as a child of five that he had had enough, looked for the maid, but not finding the maid or governess, left the crowd alone to return home. The distance from home was about two miles, and as he was returning home, he had an experience in which our Heavenly Father took him by the hand and walked him home safely. It was an unforgettable experience, and the vision was clear. Indeed, underneath are the "Everlasting Arms," and this experience gave the writer an aura of confidence, trust, and joy anytime God is mentioned because it always brings the two visions to mind that God cares, and He is dependable. Friends, readers, atheists. agnostics, apologetics, this testimony is for you to take cognizance of the existence of the God of Love that He cares for you, and whatever wrong education may have influenced you in the past, it is now time to turn around in the right direction, open a new and fresh page to see the glory of God in the face of Jesus Christ.

Testimony No. 3

This testimony is an illustration of the mighty power of God's protection in His mysterious way. A few months after being led home safely by the hand of the Most High God, our family attended another wedding of a distant relative and friend of the writer's mother. The place was an idyllic beach area of unsurpassed beauty with plants and animals of the area untouched. Being a weekend wedding, we moved into the majestic house in the area. The family must have been wealthy and the whole place was calm, cool, with salubrious wind blowing. The writer was then just nearing six years of age when he attended this magnificent wedding. The beach was one of the most beautiful beaches you can imagine, and the whole atmosphere was peaceful. The place was also a fishing village, and many canoes were anchored on the beach. While the wedding ceremony was in full swing, the writer whose name means "the fearless one," jumped into one of the canoes and paddled himself into the middle of the sea. He was easily identified as one of the wedding guests because of the clothes he had on and also because being a small fishing community and close-knit community, everybody knew everyone.

The writer remembers seeing a crowd at the beach, but the distance was far, and he could not tell whether they were in a frenzy or panic. What he remembers was two fishermen in their boar at a distance talking to him as they moved slowly but not directly towards him. They moved in parallel position so that the writer had no suspicion that the fishermen were coming for him. At a point, the fishermen appeared to stop their boat and pretended they were concentrating on their fishing. Then, gradually, they edged slowly towards the writer's boat still talking to him and gaining his confidence. When they were very close to the writer, still talking, suddenly one of them grabbed the writer and put him in their own boat. That was the mysterious way in which the writer was rescued. He could have drowned in the sea, but through the direct intervention of God, the writer was rescued. It was probably years later that the writer was able to appreciate the goodness of God and the mighty protection of the Most High God.

Testimony No. 4

During elementary school, the writer was almost always at the bottom of the class, and for three years there was little change. He was in the Baptist Elementary School when one day the teacher narrated the story of the mighty power of God in His dealings with Moses and the children of Israel and stressed the importance of prayer in the life of every believer. On that day, the writer resolved to go home and pray to the Almighty God of Abraham, Isaac, and Jacob to make him a clever and brilliant student instead of being the laughing stock of his classmates. Believing in his heart that if God has not changed, He would transform him from a dunce to a brilliant student, he prayed energetically. It was on a weekend, and he prayed sincerely over the weekend. On Monday, the teacher introduced the class to fractions in what was then called "sums" or "arithmetic." After spending a good time teaching the class with various examples, the teacher gave five problems to the class to solve. The wonder of it all was that as the teacher was explaining the techniques and methods of solving fractions and related problems, the writer understood every step, and when the teacher gave five problems to the class to solve, the writer took less than five minutes to solve all of them. He got out of his seat and presented his paper to the teacher for grading. As he got up and walked to the teacher, the class members asked whether he was finished, and he replied yes. The response triggered open laughter by all the members of the class. The dunce of yesterday suddenly had become the brain of the class. From a human standpoint, it was impossible. They remembered that only last week he was the dunce of the class and three days' gap cannot change that. That, my friends, is typical human thinking. Every pen and pencil was down, and all eyes of the class focused on the writer and the teacher. On grading his paper, the teacher became excited and announced to the class that he had gotten all the problems solved correctly. What do you think happened? The teacher could not believe but he was full of praise for his transformed student. One of the big boys and bully took the writer's pencil and pen and hastily got permission to go to the bathroom on an emergency basis. Guess what? He took the pencil and pen of the writer to the bathroom and urinated over them because he believed that the writer used Obi" or "African Juju" in his pen and the erroneous belief was that urinating over the pen and pencil neutralized the African Juju in the pen. So, the bully returned to class with a big smile on his face and told the others that he had neutralized the pen and pencil and there will be no more of that performance. However, that was a life-changing experience for the writer. His faith in God increased, and when he walked uprightly, his grading marks were always between 97% to 100% He was nicknamed "Air Mail Audy." The writer was looked upon with great suspicion by the rest of the class. However, one student came to the writer and asked for the secret of his success. The writer gave him the testimony that you have just read, and he said to the writer, "Do you mean that is all you did?" By that time, the Holy Bible had become my daily companion and every Friday was a "fasting and praying" day for the writer, but his parents did not know that he fasted every Friday. His friend asked him if he, too, who was struggling in his academic work, could be helped by the power of God. He received a triumphant answer of yes, and both of them agreed to fast and pray every Friday. Within days, the less able student became a competent and able student. Therefore, it is no secret what God can do. What He's done for others, He will do for you.

Dear readers, this testimony is for you to rest assured in God and Christ that what is impossible with men is possible with God. The friend of the writer was so gifted in mathematics, which used to be his worst nightmare, that before he graduated as a mechanical engineer, he was honorarily "knighted" as "Sir J" by his lecturer and professor as he was the student always correcting the professor when the professor was working out problems in front of the class. His understanding of mechanics and mathematics was beyond his own belief, testifying to the mighty power or God that changed him from a dunce in mathematics to a wizard in mathematics and mechanics. He eventually became an energetic minister of Jesus Christ, advertising the goodness of God in his life. It was not smooth sailing for both the writer and his friend, and there were bumps and setbacks on the journey. Both found God's words to be true in all areas. When they were walking uprightly, things went smoothly with them. When they wandered away, they suffered setback upon setback, but each time both called upon the name of God in Christ, they always found Him "a very present help in trouble." The writer and his friend, however, had become for many years separated. One went to Scotland and the other to London. While in Scotland, the writer went through a series of successes and setbacks, but the visions with revelations were spectacular, and they will encourage you.

Testimony No. 5 - Vision of God in a Flat in Scotland

The writer on this occasion lived in a room within a flat, an apartment of five bedrooms, as a student, and one day the writer received the confirmation of the truth of the word of God as contained in the Bible. Since the age of three when the writer could memorize words, the first passage he learned by memory was Psalm 1, which he was always reciting: "Blessed is the man who walks not in the counsel of the ungodly, nor stands in the way of sinners, nor sits in the seat of the scornful. But his delight is in the law of the Lord, and in His law, he meditates day and night. And he shall be like a tree planted by the rivers of water, that brings forth its fruit in its season, its leaf also shall not wither, and whatsoever he does shall prosper." The writer knew those lines from childhood but was about to witness the veracity of the Psalm. As he sat down with fellow adult students on that day in Scotland, about five people started gossiping about the sister of the landlord with many derogatory remarks, fun, and jesting. After the jesting and gossiping, everyone went to their rooms. While the writer was in his room, the vision of God appeared unto him and reprimanded him that it was wrong to gossip and to go and apologize to the sister of the landlord as soon as she returned. The vision vanished. Then it appeared that a big heavy stone was pressing the writer down on his back and chest, and he was also filled with sorrow and sadness of heart. The writer was feeling reluctant to go to the lady and tender an apology because she had not even been there, and others would not tell her what transpired at her back. Pride took over the writer's heart, but the thought of the clear vision and the uncomfortable heavy stones on his back and chest compressing and distressing him convinced him there was no way out but to obey the commandment of the Heavenly Father to go and confess everything to the lady. Summoning courage, he humbly asked for a conference with the lady and as soon as he began confessing all the things said during the "gossiping period," the big and burdensome rock on the chest and back disappeared and the writer was filled with joy and peace of mind beyond imagination, and he burst out in song of joy. Human words cannot describe the experience of God or convey the vividness and serenity of the experience.

Since that day, the writer refrains from joining a gossiping group or gossiping because it is against the guidelines of God as contained in the Holy Bible. The writer was taught directly by God to soberly share this vision of God with all. The experience taught the writer that sin is the factor responsible for sadness and sorrow in peoples' lives and because they repeat the same thing daily, they become "dead" in sin, but when they come to God through Christ and are washed spiritually by the blood of Jesus, sorrow disappears and is replaced with joy which the Bible calls "unspeakable joy."

Friends, readers, atheists, agnostics, apologetics, and all people, this vision is dedicated to you so that you can come to the only true God. He exists and rules in the lives of His children and people. There is a God of Truth who reveals Himself to all those who seek Him in sincerity and in truth. You can call unto Him now as you read these lines, and, in His mysterious ways, He will reveal Himself to you with signs and wonders. It is time to come to the God of our Peace, and He will fill you with happiness in the midst of your problems.

Do not let this opportunity slip away from you. He is waiting for your move. Invite Jesus into your heart by saying this simple prayer of faith: "Jesus, come into my heart, wash away all evil thoughts, all wrong things by your precious blood and make me a new person for God and you. Amen." Repeat this prayer silently all the time and the frequency of the prayer will generate intensity of the energy, pressure, force, and power of Christ that will come into you and give you a life-changing experience. If you are an alcoholic, you will suddenly realize that you no longer crave drinks. If you have any problem, the peace of God will enter into your heart and give you hope and assurance that all will be well. The writer can liken the rapidity of the result to a pot of water placed on an electric stove. The frequency of your prayer corresponds to the intensity of the heat energy applied to the pot of water. If your prayers are frequent, they correspond to the highest level of energy you applied and the quicker the water in the pot will boil. If you use the prayer once a day, it corresponds to the lowest level of heat energy you apply to a pot of water on the stove, and it will take a longer time for the water to boil. However, there are exceptions to the rule. That depends on God and Christ, for individuals differ and situations can be expedient and urgent and, in such situations, prayer results are like a container placed in a microwave and the contents are heated immediately. In like manner, depending on the situations of different individuals, certain prayers are answered instantaneously and border on miracles.

Dear friends, atheists, agnostics, apologetics, and all people, this is the secret of the guidelines given to us by our Lord Jesus Christ to "Pray without ceasing" because the frequency of the prayer intensifies the pressure, force, power, and rapidity of our request.

Testimony No. 6 — An Extraordinary Dream of Jesus

About forty years ago, back in Glasgow, Scotland, the writer had an extraordinary dream in which he saw the Lord Jesus Christ in all His glory with His trains of saints. The atmosphere was one that human words are inadequate to describe. The best highlighted picture that human understanding might comprehend is that of an environment of inexpressible joy, orchestrated with pomp, splendor, majesty, and magnificence beyond the imagination of mortals.

The writer was so overwhelmed that he was the one who spoke to the Lord Jesus Christ and his exact words were "Help me to preach the gospel." He awoke from the dream. Over the years, the vividness of the dream glows in the heart of the writer, and he has sought the best way to fulfill the desire to preach the gospel. Establishment of an Evangelistic Association was contemplated but ruled against because of various complications. However, in the twenty-first century, the secularism, totalitarianism, and the movement of the world toward a dictatorship of relativism which does not recognize anything as certain ignited the burning desire to testify to the absolute truth as one who has experienced the visions of God on several occasions and proclaim, through the ministry of writing this. book, the veracity of the word of God in its entirety. The writing ministry, therefore, offers the writer the greatest opportunity to preach the gospel of truth and light to all people, to share the wonderful experience of the living God and on this occasion make a special appeal to all the atheists and agnostics of the world with this message – God exists, and He rules the universe. His ways are not our ways. His thoughts are not our thoughts. He is a spirit, and He loves you. He does not want you or anyone to perish, and that is why this chapter of this book is written so that when you read about His appearances to a man in the twenty-first century, you might come to Him. In the world that we live in, there are conditions or rules to follow before you given a certificate of competency to be a mechanic, an attorney, a doctor, or any imaginable skilled profession. Aren't you happy to know that there is only one condition that God demands. That condition is to come to Him through the blood of Jesus Christ which will wash you spiritually, and you will be born again of God. Jesus Christ is the only sure and certain way back to God.

In science, any experiment performed in one part of the world, let's say Japan, can be repeated and duplicated in Europe, Russia, America, Africa, or any part of the world. If the same results are obtained when the experiment is repeated, the hypothesis is validated. In like manner, the writer invites you to use the science procedures to find out the truth yourself about the existence of God. In this scenario, you are not blindly accepting the testimony or witness of the writer, but you are like a scientist conducting an experiment to validate the successful experiment of another scientist. However, the conditions must be the same. That means you must follow the procedures step by step. It is universally accepted that science begins with observation, and the inferences we draw are the interpretations of our observations.

Before we embark upon this scientific exploration, it is essential to point out the safety rules. It is a divine violation of the Principles of God for anyone to "put God to test" because anything that is not of faith constitutes sin. It is absolutely preposterous to think or argue about the existence of God for various reasons, especially scientific reasons. Nevertheless, in order to help atheists, agnostics, and apologetics, we shall conduct a scientific experiment to reveal the "hidden God." Our hypothesis is "Does God exist in hidden form?" We shall approach our experiment not in the conventional scientific way but in a radical revolutionary way because it will enable us to grasp the gist of our work. We need background information to prepare our assignment. One of the holy names of God is "Ittami" which means "hidden", so we know from the onset that He is a "hidden God," but He has given us a promise that when we seek Him in earnestness of purpose, we shall find Him. Therefore, we are following guidelines given to us and are seeking God in earnest. Bearing this in mind, we are not putting God to test, but we are obeying His instructions to seek Him, and we are relying on His promise that we shall find Him.

Procedures:

1) You should not embark on this experiment with the attitude of skepticism or unbelief.

2) You should approach the experiment with faith because "Without faith, it is impossible to please God for he that corneal to God

must believe that God is, and He is the rewarder of them that diligently seek him" (Hebrews 11 :6).

3) You should substitute the word "sincerely" for "diligently" because if you seek God in "sincerity" you will find Him according to His promise.

Experimental Details:

Science begins with observations, and inferences are the interpretations or explanations of our observations.

Historical Precedent:

Before Moses found God. he began with observation of the environment and saw the bush burned with fire and the bush was not consumed. Undoubtedly, this is supernatural. Moses turned aside to make observations why the bush was not burnt. This shows that Moses had a scientific mind. The scriptures tell us that when Moses made the observations, God took the initiative and called unto Moses out of the midst of the bush. God reveals Himself as the Lord. The question is not whether God exists but in what form he exists. God's only begotten son who came to reveal God to us says in John 4:24 that "God is a spirit." Scientifically speaking, He is a force, the greatest force in the universe. We do not see a force or forces because they are invisible, but we see the effect of forces. We do not see the force of gravity, but we, as well as objects, encounter the force daily. Do we want to argue that because we cannot see the force of gravity it does not exist? The answer is obviously no. The force of gravity exists, but we cannot see it. In like manner, God exists, but though we cannot see Him, we do see His miraculous works all around us. The Holy Scriptures tell us that Heaven and earth is full of God and in any environment, we dare look into, we see the "Finger of God" everywhere. Dear Reader, can you understand why it is outrageous and preposterous to doubt the existence of God? God is everywhere in every imaginable environment. God is the true life of that environment.

Bearing in mind that science begins with observations and our inferences are the interpretations of our observations, let us look at three specific areas of human population to see whether by our observations we can make an acceptable scientific inference.

The human population today is over six billion. What does this mean? It means that there are over six billion individuals in the world today and each individual is unique scientifically because each individual has a specific fingerprint that is different from the rest. Only God, the unseen force and mathematician of the ages, designed each fingerprint. Of the six billion people, each individual has a specific DNA different from the rest. The DNA can be described as classified information of the life of every individual. In the DNA, we see the resounding confirmation of a God who declares the end from the beginning. The DNA has the information of every individual, and the specificity and accuracy of its information is beyond human comprehension.

Therefore, through our observations of the fingerprint and DNA in over six billion people, we see the hand of a super mathematician and scientist, and we make the inference that God is hidden in each individual and He is the unseen force and wisdom in each DNA.

The Psalmist tells us that the "Heavens declare the glory of God, and the firmament shows His handiwork." We have examined individuals in the human population. Our inference is that God exists in invisible form in each individual, and our conclusion, therefore, is that existence of God is not an exercise of Quod Erat Faciendum but a magnificent statement of Quod Erat Demonstratum. "The Lord liveth, and blessed be my rock, and let the God of my salvation be exalted" (Psalm 18:46).

No one can deny the existence of wind, and our God rides upon the wings of the wind. if you cannot see the wind, how do you expect to see God? Our God is invisible and hidden according to His holy name "Ittami".

The third specific area of scientific confirmation of the existence of God is historical in the different languages spoken by more than six billion people in the world today. Scientific survey shows that there are about 7,000 known languages spoken in the 200 countries of the world. Two thousand, two hundred and sixty-one have writing systems. The others are only spoken. The diversity of language is historical and recorded for us when God intervened in the affairs of men. We read in Genesis 11 that the whole earth was of one language and of one speech. Then the people decided to build a tower and city. Due to one spoken language, they achieved unity in purpose. However God, the living

God, confounded their language and scattered them upon the face of all the earth, and the Tower of Babel was abandoned. If one dismisses the historical account of the Tower of Babel, we might as well dismiss recorded history as unreliable. In like manner, we can question the occurrence of the First World War and the Second World War or the massacre of six million Jews by Hitler as fiction. But they are not, are they?

We have looked upon the population of man and the uniqueness of each individual with special fingerprints and DNA and drawn the inference that God exists in a "hidden form." Let us now reconsider the words of David in Psalm 19, "The heavens declare the glory of God and the firmament shows His handiwork." Astronomers tell us that the twenty-first century solar system is now complicated. Do we have nine planets or twelve planets? The definition of a planet has put the astronomers in complete disarray. At school, we learned there were nine planets: Mercury, Venus, Earth, Mars, Jupiter, Neptune, Uranus, and Pluto. The big problem for the astronomers is Pluto. Is it a planet or not? Our discoveries of the heavenly bodies validate the Holy Scriptures. We now know about comets and asteroids, the Port Cloud, the Kipper Belt, a ring of icy bodies beyond Neptune's orbit. There are also dozens of moons circling the planets. A new object nicknamed Xena has been found orbiting in the Kuiper Belt at a distance of nine billion miles from the sun. It is hailed as the tenth planet and has a moon. Have you ever wondered how the universe is put together? There will be many more discoveries and, sooner or later, the world will come to believe the immortal statement of Jesus, "In my Father's house, there are many mansions."

Therefore, our conclusion is that God exists everywhere. Indeed Heaven and earth are full of God and His glory. "Quod Erat Demonstratum."

Before bringing this chapter to a close, it is fitting to share with you the vision of God of another individual in the twenty-first century and was taught by God to count her blessings. She shared this experience with her husband. When two witnesses corroborate an account in law, their testimony is valid, and so, too, was it enacted in God's law.

Testimony No. 7 — Appearance of God the Father to a Blessed
Woman: God Cares for Us

This is a true account as related to the writer by a blessed woman. This woman is called blessed because anyone to whom God chooses to reveal Himself is a blessed individual from whatever angle we view the statement. The fact that God, the Eternal King, appeared to the woman shows that God cares for every creature. The fact that God taught this woman to count her blessings instead of moaning and being miserable is a lesson that every human being in every nation of the world should learn. The woman told the writer that everyday her husband was away to work. She was always complaining, cleaning the house and the windows in tears. On this blessed day, she was cleaning the windows and crying, moaning and miserable, when all of a sudden, she lifted up her head and saw the vision of God, the Heavenly Father who asked her why she was crying and miserable.

She replied that she cleans the windows every day and that upsets her because she alone does the cleaning of the windows. Then she told the writer, with composure, that God the Heavenly Father had asked her these questions, "Do you know how many millions of women in the world there are who have no home and would be so glad to clean the windows? Do you know many would like to be in your shoes?" When she heard these questions, she said her heart was filled with joy, and she just said, "Thank you, thank you;" and when the vision of God vanished, she became filled with joy and continued cleaning the windows happily, joyously, thankful that she's counted worthy to be taught by God the lesson of counting one's blessings. That woman is the wife of the writer. So my dear friends, readers, and people of the world, there is a God who cares for us, and we can find Him when we seek Him in sincerity and in truth.

Since this chapter is an appeal to the atheists, agnostics, skeptics, and scoffers, it is fitting to say that all the seven testimonies written about the visions and appearances of God should kindle thought-provoking actions within each individual. However, everyone should search prayerfully so as not to repeat the error of Immanuel Kant, who wrote that "the existence of God is postulate of practical reason." As such, it remains a matter of faith, not of proof. Wrong! The writer vehemently disagrees. While faith is an essential ingredient, the testimonies recorded triumphantly display the proof of God.

The Holy Scripture says God is not far from you. It is in Him that you live, move and have your being. He is nearer to you than the very eyes you see with. Call Him today, and He will answer you. He does not fail. He is faithful, just and holy.

God bless you. Amen.

Your Choice: Freedom to Choose

Friends, atheists, agnostics, apologetics, fellow travelers on this planet earth and readers, we have now come not to the end but the beginning of a new era of hope, peace, joy, tranquility, serenity, opulence, happiness, sound health and everlasting life. However, before we embark upon this boat under the captaincy of Jesus Christ, we all have a choice to make. Life is about freedom enriched with choices. Freedom and choices are twins in nature.

From the onset of life, we are given freedom enveloped in choices. It has been said that life is about choices and decisions. Making the right choices and decisions is both individualistic and collective in nature. The creator of man gives him freedom or what has been called free will. At the beginning, man was free and enjoyed his freedom for a long time before he lost his freedom. In the Garden of Eden, Adam and Eve enjoyed freedom to the fullest. However, they had a choice to make — obey the instructions of the Creator and Giver of all the good things of life they were enjoying or disobey the instructions given by the Creator. Adam and Eve used their freedom to make the wrong choice, and the wrong choice led to enslavement by Satan the devil. Enslavement cost them the loss of God, the true source of peace, happiness, joy, and sufficiency, and ushered in fear, insecurity, need, suffering, toil, poverty, disease, and murder. After the disobedience, Adam and Eve heard the voice of the Lord God walking in the garden in the cool of the day, and Adam and his wife hid themselves from the presence of the Lord God among the trees of the garden. The Lord God called unto Adam and said unto him, "Where are you?" And Adam replied, "I heard your voice in the garden and I was afraid." Enslavement to the devil through disobedience brought in fear to Adam. This fear has been passed on by Adam through his genes to all generations of men.

Fear is the harbinger of all the ills of man, the root of all the woes and sufferings of man. Fear is the first deadliest weapon of the devil after the fall of man. Fear breeds jealousy which breeds anger, and anger breeds murder. The rejection of Cain's offering brought jealousy of his brother Abel, and jealousy bred anger. His anger eventually led to the first murder committed by man when he killed his brother. Murder leads to lies, pride, and insensitivity to sin. Cain told lies to God when he said that he did not know where his brother was after he had already killed him. He was insolent, full of empty pride, and asked God the question, "Am I my brother's keeper?"

From the account of the story, we hear one of the mysteries man's science does not yet know or may not know until Christ returns. We learn that blood can speak because it has a voice. God Himself said to Cain, "The voice of your brother's blood crieth unto me from the ground." Because God rules the universe with His eternal laws, murder incurs an instantaneous curse on the murderer; hence, Cain was cursed from the earth which had opened her mouth to receive his brother's blood and, being a farmer, the ground is cursed so that it will not produce maximum yield of fruits and crops for him. He will be a fugitive and a wanderer in the earth. Anyone who refuses the divine way of God is under curse, a fugitive, prone to wander from God; but the blood of Jesus Christ has redeemed us from the curse, no longer a fugitive or stranger to the household of God but accepted as a child of the Most High God.

Fear, the first deadly weapon of the devil after the fall, still operates individually and collectively in the affairs of men all over the world. Fear breeds anxiety to man though every age since man lost God. What shall we eat? What shall we drink? How can we pay our mortgages? How do we pay our auto loans? How can we clothe ourselves? The immortal words of our Lord Jesus Christ are ringing in our ears, "Seek ye first the Kingdom of God and its righteousness and all these things shall be added unto you."

The fear of failure has caused many all over the world to commit suicide. Man does not create life and must not destroy life. The tragedy of those who commit suicide is that they were unaware of their captivity in the devil's hand; and when they thought suicide was the solution to their problems, it was the deception of Satan the devil. As they committed suicide and died, they went straight to the devil for the beginning of torment and woes. It is from lack of knowledge of God that people are destroyed and suffer. For a child of God in Christ Jesus, there is no surrender. The mountains may melt away, the seas may rise to an unprecedented level, the waves may lash fiercely. Instead, "Our faith is not subject to seasons of men, but our faith is the victory that overcomes the world."

Through fear, nations have risen against nations, and wars have been precipitated by fear. Fear has made men to build weapons of mass destruction. Fear has penetrated the hearts of men, giving them all sorts of health problems and diseases of the heart. All over the so-called civilized nations in the world, billions to trillions of dollars are spent on health-related problems. All sorts of drugs, medicines. vitamins, and herbs flood the market, each product claiming to be the best. According to recent data in the United States, medical doctors wrote more than two million prescriptions in a single year for atrial fibrillation and other heart conditions. Patients taking certain drugs rushed to the market for the quick profits but disguised as miracle cures have died from lung cancer or liver damage, have gone blind or suffered from other side effects. It appears we put profits above human lives, and we are insensitive to the pains and sufferings of the masses. "What shall it profit us if we gain the whole world and lose our own souls?" Can you imagine that in the richest nation of the world, 81.8 million Americans were without health insurance at some point from 2002-2003?

What is the root cause of all the problems of the world? The root cause of all the problems is the rejection of the truth of God. God does not change and will not bend His eternal laws that rule the universe in order to pamper than. He already demonstrated His love for man and the entire world by the gift of His only begotten son to the world so that all who believe in Him should not perish but have everlasting life. God will not compromise His holiness in order to please anyone. "Be ye holy; for I am holy" is the everlasting commandment of God; and to meet that standard, He provides man with His son Jesus Christ so that when we follow His teachings, we can attain a satisfactory standard. Dear friends, for thousands of years, God has allowed the government of man to exist, and we learn from history that man has been cruel to man. Man abandons the guidelines of God as contained in the Holy Scriptures; and the consequences have been sufferings, poverty, diseases, murders, and genocide all over the world.

It is time now for a change of direction. It is time to repent, turn away from evil, and call upon our Heavenly Father. He tells us in Jeremiah

33:3, "Call unto me. I will answer you and show you great and mighty things which you do not know." He has promised that He will be our God forever and forever; and because His promises stand steadfast and sure, let us come boldly before His presence with joy because He has not given us the spirit of bondage again to fear but the spirit of adoption as sons and daughters when we accept Christ whereby, we can cry, "Abba, Father." It is not possible for us to just come to Christ and put away evil and our weaknesses of the flesh because we are enslaved by Satan the Prince of the Air and, therefore, we need the power of the resurrection of Jesus to come into our hearts and raise us up from the death of our flesh into the glorious life of holiness in God.

Dear friends and readers, you have heard the expressions "All roads lead to Rome," and "All roads lead to God." All roads may lead to Rome, but all roads do not lead to the true God. There is only one way back to the true God, and that way is Jesus Christ because of the following facts:

1) He is the Creator of man, and He has His mark in every human being by the figure 8 pattern of the human circulatory system and the 23 pairs of chromosomes in every human being.

2) Every human being has inherited the genes of disobedience, rebellion, and death from Adam. Jesus is the only one who has the power and authority to modify and change the genes of rebellion and disobedience to make you a new creature in God and Christ. In addition, He alone has the keys of life and death in His hands. He alone will put His mark on your head so that you are sealed by His Holy Spirit, and you will rise in the Day of the Lord. Prophet Muhammad does not have that power or authority to do that. Confucius does not have that power to accomplish such a feat. Buddha does not have the authority to do that. Hinduism is so complex and diverse that it might seem that each Hindu practices his or her own religion. Nanak, the founder of the Sikhs or the Sikh religion does not have the authority or power to do that. Dalai Lama, the spiritual leader of the Tibetan people and a revered worldwide Buddhist teacher, does not have the power and authority of Jesus Christ.

3) Only Jesus was sinless and the only one "worthy of all praise."

4) Only Jesus Christ rose from the dead and holds the keys of life and death.

You see, therefore, my readers, all roads may lead to Rome, but all roads do not lead to the only true God. There is only one narrow road that leads everyone back to the only true God, the cross of Jesus Christ.

Dear friends, one of President Kennedy's famous statements is, "Do not ask what your country can do for you, but what you can do for your country." If every individual in the country turns to the God of the Hebrews, the God of Jesus Christ, the nation collectively will reap the benefits of peace because "The eternal God is our refuge and underneath are the everlasting arms." Do not be deceived any longer. All the facts are naked in your eyes. You have the inalienable right of freedom to choose, bearing in mind that whatever choice you make, there are benefits, rewards or consequences. May God help you to make the right decision and come to Jesus Christ, the answer to all human problems and woes. You can do this for your nation as a patriot. Just say the simple prayer: "Jesus, come into my heart now and make me a new creature. Amen." Welcome to the family of God.

Dear friends and readers, what is your choice? Remember that the whole Bible from Genesis to Revelation is about Jesus Christ, the Alpha and Omega, the Beginning and the End. The codes of Jesus are all around our bodies from the head to the feet. There is a meaning for everything and a reason for everything in the wisdom of God.

Please think of the following facts:

5 wounds of Jesus on the cross
5 fingers on your hands
5 toes on your feet
23 pairs (2+3) of chromosomes in your DNA, and finally
The figure 8 pattern of the human circulatory system

These facts are the reason every knee shall bow down and confess that Jesus is the Lord of all.

Dear friends and readers, we are given free will or freedom to choose. Everywhere, people are clamoring for freedom, singing "Freedom,

freedom, freedom, freedom for you, freedom for me, freedom for all, freedom to choose everlasting life or everlasting damnation!"

What is your choice?

Bibliography

Begley, Sharon. Article Title? The Wall Street Science Journal 13 May 2005.

Caner and Caner. Unveiling Islam. Kregel Publications, 2002.

"Caucasians' Skin Color is Result of Mutated Gene, Experts Say." Tampa Tribune.

16 Dec 2005.

"Children's Blood Pressure on the Rise." Tampa Tribune 5 May 2004.

Connolly, Sean. Apartheid in South Africa. Raintree Steck-Vaughn, 2003.

Collis, Bruno, M.D. Heart and Soul. Random House, Inc., 1995.

"Discovery Lifts Veil on Our Skin Tones." Science Section St.

Petersburg Times. 18 Dec 1005.

Friedman, Thomas. "The ABC's of Hatred" Times Nov 2004.

Grant, R.G. Racism: Changing Attitudes. Raintree Steck-Vaughn, 1999

Hitler, Adolf. Mein Kampf. Mariner, 1998.

The Holy Bible: King James Version. Oxford University Press, 1970.

Jordan, Rubin. The Maker's Diet. Siloam, 2004.

Kohn, Alfie. The Schools Our Children Deserve. Houghton Mifflin, 1999.

"Let's Accept the Faultline Between Faith and Science." USA Today. 16 Jan 2006.

"Mind Over Matter." Tampa Tribune 26 July 2004.

Montefiore, Simon, Sebag. Stalin: The Court of the Red Tsar. 2004.

National Geographic Magazine. May 2004.

"One God Against the gods." Creation Moments.

Pietsh, Paul. "The Mind of a Microbe." Science Digest. Oct. 1983, p. 69.

"Recollections from the Womb." Science 84 Dec 1984:84.

The Revised English Bible. Oxford University Press, 1989.

Ridley, Matt. Genome. Harper Collins, 2000.

Serway, Raymond and Faughn. Physics. Holt, and Rhinehart. 2005

Talmadge, Eric. "Ancient Japanese Religion Fading." Tampa Tribune 12 Nov 2004.

Trudeau, Kevin. Natural Cures They Don't Want You To Know About. Alliance Publishing Group, 2004.

"To Get Smarter, Be Patient: Brains May Do It For Us." St. Petersburgh Tmes. 11 Sept. 2005

"University Leaders Battle Rampant Student Drinking." Tampa Tribune Nov 2004. _

The Unseen Essential. Gills/Heartlight, 1990.

Walker, Richard. Encyclopaedia of the Human Body. D.K. Publishing, 2002.

www.ingramcontent.com/pod-product-compliance
Lightning Source LLC
Chambersburg PA
CBHW060516130626
46553CB00002B/515